The Ghosts from Mama's Club

The Ghosts from Mama's Club

Richard E. Kelly

Parker Ridge Publishing   Tucson, Arizona

Readers may contact the publisher at:
parkerridgepubs@aol.com
www.richardekelly.com

This edition was prepared for printing by
Ghost River Images
5350 East Fourth Street
Tucson, Arizona 85711
www.ghostriverimages.com

Cover and interior illustrations by Dan Sharp
www.dansharpart.com

ISBN 978-0-9795094-3-8

Library of Congress Control Number: 2012933693

Printed in the United States of America
First Edition
May 2012

10 9 8 7 6 5 4 3 2 1

What Other Authors are Saying About the Book

"*The Ghosts from Mama's Club* is riveting, educational, enlightening, inspirational, sad, humorous, and surprising. And Mr. Kelly's style and literary vocabulary is very appealing. As with his first book, *Growing Up in Mama's Club*, his recollection and commitment to research are impressive. His new book is full of gentle nuances that I particularly enjoyed. Most of all, this book is gutsy. It is self-deprecating, very brave...and fascinating."
—**Craig Bieber**, author of *Saylor's Triangle* and *The Permanent Plan*

"The author's first book, *Growing Up in Mama's Club*, was a poignant reminder of my childhood experience as a Jehovah's Witness. However, the read left me wanting to know what happened to Mr. Kelly as an adult. His new book, *The Ghosts from Mama's Club*, satisfies as each gap is thoroughly filled in, such as how he carefully planned his departure from the The Club and the effect his decision had on his marriage. Finally, he reveals how he moved on with his life, exorcising, albeit one small step at a time, every haunting ghost the Club left deep within him.
—**Joanna Foreman**, author of *Ghostly Hauntings of Interstate 65*

"Mr. Kelly's description of ghosts as that "sticky toxic residue" a child subconsciously attracts raised in a high-control religion gives a picture of "goo"—something we step in, stuff that traps us, weakens us, so that we'll have to limp back to our cult-religion again. In chapter after chapter the author shows us how people get trapped in this goo and how it harms their personal life. The most insidious and disgusting ghost is the one that trapped Mr. Kelly's sister, Marilyn. His book shows very clearly how difficult it is for a woman to break free from men who abuse."
—**Esther Royer Ayers**, author of *Rolling Down Black Stockings*

Contents

Dedication

I dedicate this book to my sister, Marilyn Faye Kelly, who was tragically murdered at age forty-nine. Her goal four years before being stabbed to death by her third abusive husband was to rid herself from the toxic residue of a religious experience that marginalized her life and the lives of many women. I've made her goal my own. I wrote this book to commemorate her valiant effort to identify and eradicate her ghosts.

Acknowledgements

Deciding *how to tell* the story you're about to read was not easy. Capturing forty-eight years of a life onto printed pages is a daunting task for a person who often writes like he talks. So I am grateful for the due diligence that my editor, Sherry Sterling, invested in this book. I also want to thank Craig Bieber, Joanna Foreman, Esther Royer Ayres, Ken Hake, George Stevens, Ron Stansell, Sharon Heller, Kathy Foster, Bob & Claire Rogers and Terri VandeVegte for helping me excise the dangling participles, flaccid sentences and awkward interrupters.

While writing this book, I also received my fair share of support and loving suggestions from Larry & Diane (Queen of the Winebirds) Davies, Joyce Hodges, Gerry Nicholson, Jackie Hendershott, Gerry & Fran Brenner, John Hoyle, Eric Swanson, Barbara Hedgepeth, Nona Dale, Carol Sagar, Ed Gutowski (one of my heroes) and friends and family who I will mention later in the book.

About the Ghosts

The ghosts I refer to in this book are metaphors for the toxic residue—dysfunctional behavior patterns—that people acquire during their time in a cult, in my case Jehovah's Witnesses. These ghosts manifest themselves in various forms. True cult believers will see the ghosts as warrior angels, championing God's truth. But individuals who decide to abandon their high-control religious experience will encounter haunting *Ghosts*, ghosts with the potential to hinder them from becoming mature and productive individuals.

In either case, the ghosts are active agents in the life of both the believers and the former believers, acting as wardens, trying to restrict actions and thoughts. Each ghost is capable of reconstituting itself in many shapes and forms in an effort to bedevil those people who try to leave the cult as well as those who have left it. The six ghosts in this book are:

The Ghost of Misinformation is the most insidious of the ghosts. It creeps into one's life in various ways, constantly affecting one's decisions, thoughts and actions. For instance, in the case of Jehovah's Witnesses, this ghost insists that one will die at Armageddon unless...

The Ghost of Separation uses shunning as its key manifestation. It also uses separation anxiety to make it difficult to bring closure to a person's cult experience.

The Ghost of Inadequacy infects its victims with the inability to think for oneself, an inability to articulate well-thought out beliefs, and a nagging feeling of inadequacy, especially by women.

The Ghost of Dependency haunts its victims with the inability to assimilate into mainstream society, a need to control and put down other people, a lack of self-control and an attraction to high-control religious groups and/or people.

The Ghost of Guilt leaves its victims constantly feeling guilty.

The Ghost of Indignation haunts people who have emancipated themselves from their past indoctrinations when they take no responsibility for going along with the rules and constraints—blaming the cult for their complicity—and obsessively trying to topple the cult.

While I tell my story in the pages ahead, I'll explain the ways in which each ghost affects the lives of those who are still manacled as well as those, like myself, who have freed themselves of those shackles. But don't forget, this is a story about real people—the good, the bad and it is what it is—and their struggles to find meaning in their lives

An Introduction

My childhood memoir, *Growing Up in Mama's Club*, evoked a variety of responses. Several reviewers wrote, "A great read, hard to put down, but it needs a sequel." This book is that sequel.

Another reviewer loved the first book but thought I fictionalized my feelings to tell a more interesting story. He clearly underestimated what can go through a child's mind when trapped in a *Cuckoo's Nest* world along with its Nurse Ratched-like rules, regulations and characters. Getting out of it is harder, as I hope my story will disclose.

For sixteen childhood years, I was bombarded with dysfunctional behavior patterns. While I walked away from Mama's Club as a young adult, some of the residue—*the ghosts*—I acquired from the experience haunted me off and on for the next forty years of my life. Two of the more daunting ghosts were:

The Ghost of Misinformation

13

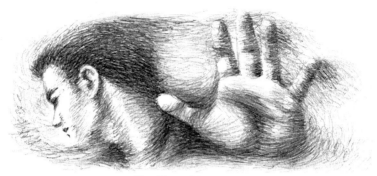

The Ghost of Separation

If those ghosts had not been identified and eventually exorcised, they could have been toxic and debilitating—mental roadblocks to leading a full, happy life after leaving a high-control religious group.

If you read my first book, you know that I grew up in a family ruled by a highly opinionated, alpha mother who believed the imminent end of the world would occur in her lifetime. So resolute and extreme were those apocalyptic convictions that Mama iron-willed survival at Armageddon as the focal point for our day-to-day life.

I had just turned four when Mama's religious conversion occurred, a five-month textbook procedure—to family and friends it seemed like an intellectual lobotomy. From her baptism until I was old enough to leave home, she relentlessly evangelized her convictions on me. At times, she could be very convincing, having no doubts about God's intention to destroy the world and nonbelievers before I reached manhood.

God's Going to Destroy Dickie at Armageddon Unless...

While I wanted to please Mama, I had my doubts about her strange beliefs. So I lived two lives—feigning belief to appease her, or escaping, when I could, into a fantasy world. At age twenty, I ended the charade and freed myself from Mama's misguided beliefs. But again, I was naïve about the toxic residue—the ghosts—that I had clandestinely closeted in my subconscious mind.

I start my story at a very special time and place, a vacation in Tuscany. Tuscany is where this book was incubated and it is the home of the Renaissance, a fitting symbol for my life.

Celebrating in Tuscany
Chapter 1

Perhaps it was the Chianti with its seductive ripe blackberry character, dark chocolate aftertaste, and long finish that influenced our decision. It may have been the full-bodied Brunello with its intense concentration of berry, chocolate, and coffee character. Whatever the source, that night in the summer of 2005, as my lovely wife and I enjoyed a leisurely dinner with good wine, we decided to reward ourselves with a big celebration. It had been a long ordeal, but I'd just completed writing and publishing the first edition of my book about growing up a Jehovah's Witness—*Mama's Club*.

However, not until we had our third glass of wine, another Brunello, with enticing aromas of very ripe fruit, fresh-cut flowers, strawberry, and cherry that we decided to make it happen in Tuscany.

After investigating several vacation homes on the internet, we decided to rent a 17th century, rural, ten-acre property—Villa Casa Bianca, in Noce, of Tavarnelle Val di Pesa. Its five large bedrooms would allow us to share the experience with our children and granddaughters. And the stately villa, perched on top of a hill overlooking the Pesa Valley, was conveniently located twenty miles south of Florence and twenty miles north of Siena.

Our celebration officially began when we landed at the Florence airport on June 17, 2006. An hour later, we drove our rented car onto the villa grounds, where we were rewarded with the sight of a huge, two-story castle. Gift-wrapped in spring green, burnt-red, and iridescent-gold creeping ivy, it oozed quintessential Italian architecture.

Our vacation home and surrounding property were well-positioned on a picturesque grassy knoll on the center of a high hill. A pastoral centerpiece, it provided a panoramic view of serene undulating hills and valleys that meander on and on as far as the eye can see. Countless rows of shimmering green vineyards twisted in all directions. Sandwiched between small groves of gray-green olive trees were splashes of tall, wavy golden-brown grasses and old stone homes with fables etched in their mortar. Capping the end of every day, a big, silky blue sky hovered high above with the one and only orange-red Tuscan sun as the centerpiece.

The celestial haze, which permeates the horizon as the Tuscan sun sets, casts a mystical spell on the landscape—a surreal mixture of light, hues, and shapes. The first time I experienced this phenomenon, I had an overwhelming sense of déjà vu. It took me awhile, but then I remembered a third-grade field trip to a Los Angeles art museum, one Mama would not have approved. There I saw paintings by an 18th century Dutch artist who captured on canvas the scenes unfolding before my eyes. A soul-stirring moment indeed, admiring this awe-inspiring landscape with my wife, children, and grandchildren.

I had come a long way, over fifty years, from a highly controlled, dysfunctional childhood. A world where artistic expression, science, sports and critical thinking were labeled tools of the Devil. Mama thought these petty indulgences robbed glory from God. That I would be here in this region where the Renaissance— the Age of Enlightenment—originated was sweet, poetic justice.

But the long journey that brought me to Tuscany did not come about smoothly. I encountered many roadblocks along the way. While my age of enlightenment officially began in the spring of 1964, it started at ground zero with all odds against me.

18

Breaking the News to Helen
Chapter 2

To initiate my renaissance, I planned to dissociate myself as one of Jehovah's Witnesses—what I will refer to repeatedly as The Club or JWs. The difficulty with my plan is that I first had to leave Bethel, the Club's worldwide headquarters. Located in Brooklyn, New York, Bethel is where Club policy is formulated, literature printed and missionaries trained. Non-paid worker bees like me manned the kitchen, laundry and printing factory.

I had lived at Bethel for fourteen months and decided to leave. But I didn't want to be alone. So on a two-week vacation in the summer of 1963, I asked Helen Joan Geerling at her Michigan home if she would marry me. Not right away, as I needed to find a well-paying job and a place to live. When I hinted that it might be in New York City, she liked the idea, although she needed to know why I wanted to leave Bethel early.

We had talked about marriage before when I was eighteen, Helen twenty. I lived at home with my parents and didn't have a full-time job. We discussed no specifics and no engagement. Then I received an invitation to work at Bethel. I liked the idea of learning new work skills and escaping from Mama's high-control. My plan, which Helen approved, was to stay four years at Bethel before making wedding plans. Now I was proposing to leave Bethel early, although I didn't know exactly when.

I told her that staying much longer at Bethel wasn't an option given my concern with the double standards and blatant hypocrisy manifested by the men in charge. The Club, governed by cold, indifferent old men, often made vindictive personnel decisions. The president, Nathan H. Knorr, verbally bullied other Bethelites. Vice President Freddy Franz lived in the past, disconnected from reality. Heavy drinking was commonplace among the leaders and the rank and file. And I had never heard the f-word used so much. I did not believe God directed this group. In fact, if I had a chance of finding spiritual contentment, I was certain it wasn't going to happen at Bethel.

This news did not come as a big surprise to Helen. She had heard rumors about unruly behavior from people at her Kingdom Hall—relatives of Bethelites. But like many Club members, she rationalized these excesses. The church leaders were imperfect men trying to please God. Jehovah would address these shortcomings in His due time. At the end of the day, it was still *the truth*, although she acknowledged that it may be time for me to leave Bethel. So she accepted my conditional marriage proposal.

I had finally told Helen something about my disenchantment with the Club and she didn't shoot the messenger. That's what Mama would have done. Helen's reaction was a good sign and I thought about telling her what I had learned about the sordid history of the Club's first two presidents, how policies and doctrines were formulated, and that actually I had never believed Club dogma. I also thought about telling her how I wanted to believe and went through the motions to please Mama. But I decided to wait. When the time was right, Helen would understand. She just needed a little more time. Hopefully, when she learned what I knew about the Club, she would leave it with me.

My biggest problem was that I didn't know what I believed because of misinformation, one of the ghosts that would haunt me for many years. When you're trapped in a cult as a child, you're swamped with massive amounts of bad information and not allowed to research alternative belief systems. Had I tried to investigate different religions, my inquiries would have repulsed Mama more than if I had told her I was researching the pros and cons of incest, bank-robbing or cannibalism. Jehovah's Witnesses often seem paranoid and obsessive-compulsive about losing their own faith and about their children becoming nonbelievers.

The Ghost of Misinformation

The Ghost of Misinformation is a daunting ghost. While I had filtered out the obvious, I had nonetheless acquired prodigious amounts of *information that ain't so*. And since I did not yet fully know what I didn't know, this skewed what little I did know about the world, myself, other people, the arts, science, history, politics and especially religion.

After returning to Bethel, I went to see two of my ex-JW friends, Bert and Charley. I told them about my plans and asked for their advice. Bert, in his early forties, prided himself as a street-savvy building-maintenance businessman. He had been an active JW, but he often summed up that experience with, "I left that shit years ago." A very smart guy, he dressed down to make people think he was struggling financially. Charley, his business partner, had worked with me in the Bethel kitchen and we'd become good friends. Charley, two years older than me and out of Bethel six months, liked to make people think he was their worst nightmare. But I knew better. Underneath the rough exterior, he had the proverbial heart of gold.

After explaining to Bert and Charley what I wanted to do, they were very supportive. Almost immediately, Bert said I could work for them in their Brooklyn Heights apartment building custodial business, starting anytime I wanted. The offer tempted me. We would have made an interesting but odd-looking team, I a foot taller than both Bert and Charley. But as much as I liked them and their offer, I knew it wouldn't work in the long term. I had different aspirations and wanted my independence. I would bide my time for the right opportunity.

In January 1964 Bert told me about a real estate mogul, Mr. Kay. Bert had worked for him before and respected him as an honest business man. In fact, James Baldwin, the famous black writer, lived in one of his buildings. Mr. Kay needed a superintendent for six ten-family apartments he owned in West Manhattan. I called him and scheduled an interview. He liked me, but thought I might be over qualified for the job. I told him about my unique circumstances and that I wanted him to meet my fiancée, which turned out to be the missing piece to his offer for the job.

I called Helen and she scheduled a three-day visit to the City. Since I still worked at Bethel, I arranged for her to stay in the home of a JW family that I knew. Less than a week after my successful job interview, I excitedly waited to greet my future wife at Grand Central Station. I nearly swooned when I first sighted her gift-wrapped in a bright red winter coat and wearing a beaming smile. My Miss America making her grand entrance.

During our first alone time, we revisited our summer conversation about my concerns with the Club. I again asked her to marry me, showing Helen for the first time his-and-her wedding rings that I had purchased for a hundred dollars.

When Helen met Mr. Kay, he apologized profusely. Our apartment wasn't available for viewing. He didn't know when we could see it, although he assured us that it was only a matter of time. A week after Helen left, he called Bert to tell me that our ground-floor studio apartment would be ready for occupancy in March. I could come see it anytime. With that news, Helen and I set the wedding date for April 11. Now for the next part of my plan, to tell the Club president, Nathan H. Knorr, I planned to leave Bethel.

I slept well the night before. I calmly worked kitchen duty the next morning, watching carefully to see when Knorr stood up after the breakfast meal ended. That was his signal that if you wanted to talk with him, now was the time to do it. When he started pulling away from the table, I moved quickly toward him and asked if I could schedule time to talk. Up close, he stood tall, a big-boned man with an imposing aura—a white George Foreman, who did not smile. He gave me a stern look, crossed his arms, and rudely stated that now was as good a time as any. I noticed that several people stopped to look, no doubt curious why I was speaking to Knorr.

Without a hint of nervousness, I announced, "I want you to know that I will be leaving Bethel in two weeks, and I'd like to tell you why."

He never looked happy, but now he ratcheted up his already harsh demeanor. He glared and tauntingly inquired, "So, why *are* you leaving?"

He was interrogating me and it suddenly unnerved me! But I stayed calm. "Because I want to get married and ...."

He held up his big right hand—his cue for me to stop and to listen. "So after you're married for a few years, do you think that you will leave your wife as well? Perhaps you will tire of her like you have of Bethel service. I wonder if you know anything about keeping commitments."

The Ghost of Dependency Likes to Maintain Total Control

I had come to Bethel to get away from Mama's put-downs and guilt trips. Now it was the High Priest of Bullies trying to work his ministerial magic. What was my big sin? Leaving Bethel before my four years were up. Wow! Good thing I didn't tell Mr. Need-to-Control what I really thought about the Club. Who knows how worked up he would have become. Unwilling to be bullied, I decided not to respond to his accusation and politely said, "I've learned a lot at Bethel and I'm grateful for that experience."

Knorr responded with a piercing Dick Cheney stare and waited for me to say something stupid. I didn't take the bait. Instead, I smiled, turned, and slowly walked away. When I finally reached the swinging kitchen doors, a rite of passage for me, I felt no pain, with my self-esteem at an all-time high.

The euphoria of knowing that I had set in motion a plan to free myself from the constraints of Mama's severe religious beliefs produced a long-lasting rush, helping my final two weeks at Bethel pass quickly. I breezed through my work and attended no Club meetings. I had stopped participating in the door-to-door ministry several months before. When I had free time, I cleaned and remodeled our one-room apartment on West 68th Street, our new home, and counted the days before Helen would join me.

Monday morning, March 30, I closed, for the last time, the large glass entrance door to the Club's headquarters. Carrying a weatherworn Salvation Army suitcase, I marched triumphantly to the St. George station, descended the graffitied concrete steps, and wove my way underground to a new life in New York City.

My destination was a cozy 480-square-foot studio apartment, located on the ground floor, street side of a five-story, ten-family brownstone. The floorboards in the 350-square-foot living room were my pride and joy. I had labored twenty-five intermittent, back-breaking hours to sandblast, stain, and varnish a hundred-year-plus hardwood floor, completing it a mere three days earlier. I must have removed a century of crud, nasty scratches and serious neglect before applying a mahogany stain and three coats of high gloss lacquer to the semi-smooth wood surface.

The living room furniture consisted of a brand new Castro-convertible couch with a queen-sized mattress. The couch's bright orange fabric served as an accent color for the newly painted off-white plaster walls. Completing the living room ensemble were two chairs, end tables, lamps, a chest of drawers, and a bookcase. All of the furniture had been abandoned by and rescued from more affluent neighbors. A sturdy ironing board did double duty as a dining room table. Conspicuously lacking was a television.

Well-worn, but clean, yellowed black-and-white linoleum covered the kitchen floor and counter. The tiny sink, freshly painted cupboards, a two-burner stove and oven, and a three-foot high refrigerator would have been spartan by today's standards. But it worked for me. A massive metal door with a triple-bolted lock system occupied most of the wall space on the west side of the kitchen. On the east side, a solid wood door provided privacy to a small bathroom tiled in black, white, and pink.

As the building superintendent—super—for the brownstone where I lived, along with five additional buildings, I juggled trash cans in and out for pickup six days a week, cleaned hallways, swept the sidewalks, and resolved small maintenance problems. Unlike at Bethel, I received compensation for my work. And if I wanted, I could add to my income by painting—twenty-four hours a day, if so inclined.

I embarked on a painting marathon, ten to twelve hours a day, for my first eleven days in the Big Apple. I earned over a thousand dollars, lots of money in those days. When I left for the airport Friday morning, I excitedly looked forward to sharing this new life, a new big city world, with Helen.

Upon my arrival at the Detroit airport, Helen greeted me with her engaging smile and open arms. But she wasn't alone. Her tall, lanky father, dressed in a tan janitor-like uniform stood proudly by her side. I had expected Helen to be alone and except for their Geerling smiles, they looked mismatched. I noticed for the first time his bald egg-shaped head. While surprised to see him, it didn't take me long to embrace the opportunity to get to know him better on our drive back to Helen's home in Holland, Michigan.

Helen had been noncommittal about her father not being a Jehovah's Witness, and I didn't know if that bothered her. But that wasn't the case with her mother, Gertrude—a dyed-in-the-wool convert—who had been very vocal about the disparity, calling Henrik a stubborn nonbeliever behind his back. For the life of her, she couldn't understand why he didn't accept her religion as *the truth*. I later learned that she thought my addition to the family would help Henrik see the light—to have him somehow love Jehovah God as she did. But Hank, as his friends called him, had a mind of his own.

Hank immigrated to this country from the Netherlands at three years of age, the youngest of four children. When his father couldn't find work in Holland, Michigan, the family moved to Alberta, Canada. They scraped out a living by farming for the next seven years. His family moved back to Holland when Hank turned eleven. Several months later, he lost his mother and sister to the Spanish influenza. A survivor, proud of his Dutch heritage and accent, he was not the kind of person who could be shamed into believing something that made no sense to him. He did not interfere with his wife's religious beliefs and expected her to treat him with the same courtesy.

Hank seemed as pleased to see me as Helen. He even asked me to call him "Pop" before chauffeuring us to his Holland home in a well-maintained Studebaker. He was proud of his car and he spent lots of time keeping it in good running shape. Gertrude had once commented about her concern for the attention he squandered on it. She thought his free time would have been better spent on supporting the heavenly Kingdom that God inaugurated in 1914—a theocratic government that now ruled our planet. Gertrude had told Helen's dad many times that God's Kingdom triggered World War I. But he didn't buy it. Gertrude believed that under the leadership of its newly ordained king, Jesus Christ, God planned to destroy this old world at Armageddon. She believed it would happen in her lifetime and that unless she toed the mark, she would be destroyed too.

The Ghost of Misinformation Reporting that You Will Die at Armageddon Unless…

During our three-hour drive to Holland, Helen briefed me for the first time on details for our wedding and reception. Since long distance phone calls were very expensive, she had planned everything on her own.

When we finally pulled into the driveway, I was very tense, but not because of Helen's wedding plans. Pop's driving skills were awful. Several times he swerved into the lane of oncoming traffic while trying to maintain eye contact with Helen or me. He couldn't hold down the gas and talk at the same time, and he constantly tapped on the brakes, as if not quite sure they would work. While I believed his inability to accept the Club's doctrines a good omen for me, I wondered if he had a death wish, especially given that Pop, a nonbeliever, was married to a fanatical religious zealot.

After exiting Pop's Studebaker, my parents and three siblings greeted me. They had driven from Nebraska to attend the wedding, arriving the night before. However, one of the first things they reported on was the three hours they spent that morning preaching in the door-to-door work with Helen's mother and sister. This act of evangelizing and then verbally reporting it, now ingrained in their religious psyche, reconfirmed to other hard-core believers how much they loved Jehovah.

As I reflect today on this peculiar behavior, I know how strange this must seem to someone unfamiliar with Jehovah's Witnesses. My parents had driven 700 miles on Thursday for their son's wedding on Saturday. They were tired and could have spent the morning getting to know Helen's father and mother. Instead, they decided to score points with God by preaching for Him from door-to-door, an affront to Helen's dad. But it helped explain why he had gone with Helen to pick me up at the airport.

Shortly after we arrived, Helen's mother fixed snacks and sandwiches. At first, we exchanged perfunctory small talk as we nibbled, but Gertrude's and Mama's need to talk about how deeply committed they were to the Truth—Club members call it *the Truth*, I call it *The Club*—took precedence. Finally, they started talking on about how much time they spent studying the Bible and evangelizing others—time spent helping other people love Jehovah as much as they did. This kind of talk ritualized their strong belief that "Faith without works is dead". (James 2: 26)

I had almost forgotten about this kind of talk at meals. At

Bethel, this game was verboten. If you persisted in this kind of talk working for Karl Hoppe in the kitchen, he would tell you in his strong German brogue that it was not the time and place for it. He believed strongly that you showed how devoted you were to God by how hard you worked. At Bethel, you wasted valuable energy boasting about your relationship with God.

However, away from Bethel that's how JW zealots played the game. Mama and Gertrude were masters at this ritual. After a few minutes, Pop started fidgeting with discomfort and excused himself, reporting that he heard the carburetor knocking slightly on our trip back. He wanted to check on it.

That was my cue. Winking at Helen, I stood up and excused myself, saying I needed to talk with Pop. He was peering under the hood on the Studebaker when I walked in. He looked up and smiled, pleased that I had joined him. We made small talk and joked before I asked, "Well, I suspect it's a little late to be doing this, but I was hoping I could go through the formality of requesting your daughter's hand in marriage."

"That's nice," he replied. "If Helen is happy, so am I."

"Well, do you have any advice?"

"Yes. Yes. Yes, I do. I love my daughter. I love all of my kids. But Helen is special. She's my ballerina. She's been pirouetting through life since she was a little girl. She loves life and her happiness is contagious. That's Helen, and she's not going to change." Then he awkwardly pirouetted a full turn before he started laughing.

This was a side of him that I had never seen before and I didn't know how to respond. What was he telling me? Generally, I'm pretty good at picking up nuances in conversation or unusual behavior, but I did not know what to make of this. I stayed quiet for a while before he broke the silence, "So Dick, would you help me clean the gas filter?"

Later that evening, we attended the dress rehearsal for the wedding at the Kingdom Hall rather than in Helen's family's living room, where the wedding was to take place the next day. While only the immediate families were invited, we rehearsed at the Hall because Gertrude didn't want to rearrange the furniture twice or track in extra dirt. And why weren't we getting married at the poorly painted Kingdom Hall that Helen, her sister and Gertrude attended in Holland, when it was big enough to accommodate extended family members? Because Gertrude was embarrassed that it once had been the home of a small unpopular Pentecostal church group.

It was close to midnight before Helen and I had an opportunity to be alone. She glowed. The official, legal beginning of our life journey together would start in a few hours, and yet, it seemed like we had way too much to talk about before saying our vows. We were also apprehensive about having sex for the first time, what with both of us being virgins! We had kissed and touched passionately several times before, but we had always stopped going all the way, very aware of the consequences of sex before marriage. Oh my, how the Ghost of Pervasive Guilt would have haunted us then.

The Ghost of Guilt

To Jehovah's Witnesses, premarital sex ranks as a major no-no. We were constantly reminded from talks at the Hall and articles in *The Watchtower* that it was fornication, one of the most heinous crimes you could commit in the eyes of God. If, in a wild act of passion, we had gone all the way, we would have been obligated to report our sin against the Holy Spirit to a three-man committee of elders. They would have wanted to hear the details about the act, including whether full penetration had been achieved, how many times we did it, if we had oral sex and how repentant we were.

After the interrogation, the elders would document their find-

29

ings, recommend an appropriate punishment—excommunication or probation—send their report to the Club headquarters for approval, and wait. When the elders received the official notice, the breaking news would be reported at a Thursday night meeting. If Helen and I were the offenders, our identity and sin would be reported at the Halls we attended. If contrite, we would attend that meeting. Fortunately, our history did not play that way.

Our wedding and reception were rather uneventful. I thought the best part of the experience would come late that evening. However, when the moment arrived, we were exhausted. But not too tired to embrace celibacy for another day. The short, unexciting consummation took place at the Ship & Shore Motel on the Kalamazoo River in Saugatuck, a resort town fifteen miles from Holland.

The next morning we met our families at Helen's old home for lunch. After packing the car, we said our goodbyes and embarked on a honeymoon drive to a new life and our new home in New York City. But not just in any car, we cruised to a new chapter in our life in a chariot—Helen's four-door, salmon-and-white, mint-condition 1957 Chevrolet—a classic today.

I had good intentions to tell Helen about my big decision to leave the Club, and why, on our drive to the City. Somehow, the right moment never materialized. As we neared our destination, I decided to wait to tell her after we were settled in, confident she would understand.

Tim's Surprise Visit
Chapter 3

We arrived at our apartment late in the day on Monday. As I searched for a place to park, the excitement of sharing my new home with Helen for the first time consumed me. She had never seen the place—not even a picture. While we had luggage and wedding gifts to bring in, that would have to wait. First, I wanted to carry her over the threshold. Then I wanted—no, I needed—to know that she approved of her new home. It didn't take long to find out, when she christened the sparkling spartan apartment with, "It's perfect. You couldn't have given me a better gift."

On Tuesday the next day, while I did my morning chores, Helen stayed in bed. A light dusting of snow covered the ground and the early morning cool intensified my tingling I'm-not-a-virgin-any-longer senses. I was a married man and life was very good, living in a dream world. When I arrived home, Helen—bathed and dressed as scantily as possible—suggested that I shower and join her in bed. Our first night in Saugatuck doing the real thing wasn't what we expected, the second night in Toledo wasn't much better. But we knew with indulgent persistence we'd figure it out. We were on the second go-around when the intercom buzzer startled us. I jumped out of bed, pushed the intercom button, and asked, "Who is it, please?"

"It's Tim. Can I come in?"

While it took a moment to comprehend the request, I did not reply subtly. "Tim, walk around the block two times and come back."

His delay in comprehension lasted longer than mine. When it

finally dawned on him, he said, "See you in ten minutes."

Helen jumped out of bed and while dressing, asked, "What do you think your brother wants this time of day?"

My brother, Tim, lived at Bethel, his home for over a year. Two weeks before, he had traveled to see my parents in Nebraska and rode with them to our wedding. I neglected to ask what his travel plans were en route back to the city. We'd been Bethel roommates my last year, but we seldom talked and I never confided in him. While I knew he observed the hypocrisy and double standards at Bethel, he had never shared his innermost thoughts.

"Helen, I haven't a clue. I didn't know he was back in the City."

In today's world you wouldn't think about visiting a friend or family member without a telephone call beforehand or an invite. However, this was a much different time. We had a telephone in our apartment paid for by my employer, but for local calls only. Tim had access to a pay phone in the lobby at Bethel, but people only used it if their parents had money. Tim definitely couldn't afford to use the phone.

When the intercom buzzed the next time, I pushed the button, allowing Tim to enter the hallway. I opened the door to our apartment and Tim greeted me with a big toothy grin, unable to feign ignorance about what we'd just been doing. We shook hands and I invited him in. Helen had coffee perking and asked if he wanted something to eat.

"Dick and Helen, I'm sorry to barge in like this. But I need to talk with you. I think I'm in love."

"Who's the lucky girl?" Helen asked.

"It's your sister, Esther."

Helen and I looked at each other in amazement. Esther had been Helen's maid of honor and Tim my best man at our wedding. They had spent parts of three days together. So what could have happened in that short period of time? Tim, now nineteen, had never been on a date before. I wasn't sure that he had any interest in sex. Had I underestimated him?

Then it dawned on me. People were regularly reminded at Bethel, in *The Watchtower*, and at meetings that if they are constantly feeling horny, they should get married. Masturbation and sex outside of marriage were not acceptable options if JWs wanted to stay in the good graces of the Club.

Tim wanted to leave Bethel in a year and get married. He was certain that Esther was the right girl, that she liked him as well. But he wanted advice on courting. He also asked if he could do odd jobs for me when he wasn't working at Bethel. He had had little sleep in the last twenty four hours due to an all-night bus ride from Detroit, although that was hard to tell with his uncharacteristic animation. Wondering if he might be thinking about leaving the Club, I asked what he planned to do and where he would live.

"I'd like to move to west Michigan, to be closer to Esther's family. My goal is to *pioneer* (a person who spends 100 hours a month in the door-to-door ministry), both of us. I've never liked it at Bethel and I don't want to end up like so many bitter, unhappy Bethelites who spend their lives doing work they don't enjoy. You know how cold the people are there. I know it's Jehovah's organization; it's just not the place where I want to spend the rest of my life."

So he wasn't thinking about leaving the Club after all. He had seen what goes on at Bethel and formed a totally different opinion about his experience than I had. Tim was a true believer and proud of his religious beliefs even if he hadn't actively participated in formulating them. They were Mama's beliefs and Tim was honor-bound to accept them as his own without question.

Not that my religious beliefs reflected any serious, deep thinking. Frankly, it would take me many years before I could articulate well-thought-out beliefs about God, life after death and the Bible.

The Ghost of Inadequacy Makes it Difficult to Articulate Well-Thought-Out Beliefs

33

However, I knew precisely what religious beliefs I didn't accept. But, Helen's positive response to Tim's pioneering plans convinced me that I had to talk with Helen right away.

Tim had taken the time to find out where the nearest Kingdom Hall was located, and showed us the Hall's location on a map. He reported that the two one-hour Sunday meetings started at 1:00 PM and 2:15 PM; Tuesday's one-hour book study met at 8:00 PM; and the two-hour Thursday meetings started at 7:30 PM. Tim said that Fred Rusk served as the congregation servant—the presiding minister. He then explained to Helen that Fred was also a full-time professor at Bethel's Gilead—a six-month school for Club missionaries. Ironically, Fred personified the unhappy, rude, cold Bethelites Tim did not want to become.

I had mixed feelings about Fred. On the one hand, he had been supportive of me during the six months I spent in Primary—a special school that all new Bethelites are required to attend. The curriculum was designed to evaluate each individual's potential to rise in the Club hierarchy. Fred had been one of three instructors who had given me good marks for my learning and speaking skills. But he and his wife, Marge, were nitpickers. They constantly complained about the meals at Bethel. The food was too cold or too spicy, not enough salt, or overcooked. And, for the two years I served at Bethel, I never saw Fred smile. He was a consummate loner, even though he was married.

I now knew from the conversation with Tim that Helen planned to go to the meetings and participate in the door-to-door work. She wouldn't walk away from the Club with me in the short term. But I had new urgency to tell her about my plans to leave and that I was not a believer. I also wondered for the first time what Fred Rusk would tell Helen when she told him I wanted to leave the Club and why.

Club members are programmed to tattle on fellow members with that kind of information. Helen would do it, although she would never think of it as tattling. The Club frames it as information that needs to be shared in order to keep the organization pure. What would Fred think when Helen told him that I had lost my faith? It wouldn't take long to find out, although it didn't turn out to be what I had imagined.

Helen's Response
Chapter 4

With Tim barely out the door of our apartment, Helen abruptly turned to face me. "So, you haven't attended a meeting or gone in the door-to-door work since you left Bethel, have you?"

Before I could say a word—a "no" easily explained—she asked, "When do we go to our first meeting? What are Fred Rusk and his wife like? Didn't Tim say Brother Rusk was a Gilead instructor?"

"Whoa!" I replied, knowing now wasn't the time. I didn't want to answer these questions without first telling my story. Tim's visit had not been planned and a painting project beckoned. So I asked, "Can we talk about this after dinner?"

Helen liked the idea. In fact, she wanted to explore the neighborhood while I worked. This would be the first dinner at our new home, and she planned to make it special. Our plan to talk later would give her plenty of time to shop and prepare the meal.

After finishing my painting project, I stopped at the store to buy two quarts of Miller High Life, which I gift-wrapped in a brown bag. However, when I unlocked the door and walked into the apartment, a thick gray haze greeted me and then the sickening smell of what I imagined as badly burned beef kidney. Helen stood at the stove crying. She had bought two large lamb chops from the butcher shop and pan fried them like steaks, but with no marinade or special prepping. When she first smelled the strange odor, she thought it would go away if she cooked the meat longer.

I took this opportunity to shine. While she aired out the apartment, I whisked the stinky meat into a trash can outside and rushed to the grocery store. There I bought the best ground sirloin I could find. I also purchased another bottle of beer. Two would not be enough.

Evidence of the gamey meat still lingered when I arrived home, but the aroma of top-grade hamburger meat mixed with generous chunks of garlic and onion cooking on the stove quickly erased it. Adding a skillet of fried potatoes and more onions, the steamy scents now promised comfort. The fact that the cook and her husband drank beer during the cooking experience didn't hurt. Helen's trademark smile and laugh returned, making the dinner a big success.

After we washed dishes, cleaned the kitchen, and folded up the ironing board table, I initiated the overdue conversation. "Helen, I can't tell you how happy I am in this new life. Sure, we had a small mishap this evening. Those things are going to happen. What I like is that we're doing it together. I want to be there when you need me and I hope you'll always be there when I need help. That's why what I'm about to tell you is so important. I feel for the first time in my life that I can be totally honest with myself. And I want to be the same with you."

"I know, Dick. It's a dream come true. Here we are together in this big city. It's all so exciting."

"Helen, we're embarking on a long journey together. I don't know where we'll go or what lies ahead but I think for it to work, we have to be open and honest with each other all the way."

I stopped and thought how to best start what I had to say. Then I began slowly, "Bethel was a bittersweet experience for me. On the one hand, I wouldn't be where I am today—married to you, working and living in New York City, or feeling like I could conquer the world—without my time there. But I also saw the worst of what religion does to people there. No, I'm not naïve; I saw lots of it growing up, as well."

I took a deep breath. Now the hard part: "The real problem is that I've never been convinced that Jehovah's Witnesses have the truth. While I wanted to believe, it never happened. I told Mama many times about my doubts, but she'd put these guilt trips on me, so I quit trying.

"I learned to tell her what she wanted to hear. I did it with other Jehovah's Witnesses and with you at times. Now that has to change. I have to be honest with you if this marriage is going to work. My biggest concern is that I don't know what I believe. But, I know for sure the Watchtower Society doesn't have a monopoly on the truth, as it boasts to its members."

It wasn't going well. I could see it in her eyes. Light tears slowly inched down her face. So I stopped and waited.

"What are you saying? That you never believed it? Were you just leading me on until we got married? Why couldn't you have told me this a few months ago?" Then she waited.

These were good, tough questions, and I immediately regretted waiting so long before telling her. Then it suddenly occurred to me that I could reframe the conversation. It would buy me time. So I nervously said, "Listen, I'm trying to be honest, as I hope you'll be with me. I'm not going to meetings or in the door-to-door work for thirty days. Then, we'll see where I am. But in the meantime, you attend the meetings and go door-to-door if that's what you think is right."

Bingo! It was apparent that framed this way, I had provided Helen with some wiggle room. She was processing information much differently now. It would take me several years to learn that Helen, like most people, does not react quickly to information that flies in the face of what she knows to be so, that ain't so. She needs time to think it over, to process it. Again, there was a long pause before she grabbed my hand and said, "Dick, I love you. I know it was difficult for you at Bethel. I think you need a break. It will be good for you to take the time off."

The mood changed dramatically. I desperately wanted to ask her to join me in my moratorium. However, I knew at this point in time, she saw meeting attendance as a reflection of her loyalty to God. If she stopped, that would have meant giving in to temptations from the Devil. That's how her conscience was trained—part of the Club's 24/7 control: We do your thinking for you. Helen's ability to mentally process why attending a Club meeting put God first in her life had been chiseled away and replaced with Club misinformation. So she easily made the decision to go to the Thursday meeting, two days away.

Unable to Think for Oneself is a Symptom of the Ghost of Inadequacy at Work

While I worked the next morning, Wednesday, Helen called the Kingdom Hall. Connie, a young, single African-American woman answered. It didn't take the two of them long to connect. They were sisters with common beliefs, spiritual soulmates, in spite of the fact that they were perfect strangers. This phenomenon is frequently touted as one the unique trademarks of the Club, something you don't see in other religious groups. Or at least that's what Mama used to tell me.

If you were a member of the Club and lived in California and were stranded in Chicago, you could call someone at a local Kingdom Hall. Once connected, you'd be treated as an honored relative. No denying that this sometimes happens, but more often than not, those people who asked for help looked for a handout. These were Club members who knew how to work the system. I knew the Club didn't have a monopoly on this kind of generosity. Other religious groups, Mormons to name one, would do the same thing. But still, Mama refused to believe it.

Helen didn't ask Connie for a handout; she wanted to talk. New to the area, recently married, she needed a listening ear. Connie said that if Helen had the time, she could be at our apartment in thirty minutes. It happened that quickly. When I picked up supplies at noontime, two hours had passed and they were talking like long-lost friends. When Helen introduced me, my doubts about the Club had not been discussed. In fact, Connie treated me as if I was a high ranking Bethelite.

She gushed on and on about how pleased she was to have Helen and me going to her Kingdom Hall, how she knew we'd get along with her friends, how we had a lot in common. Connie seemed like the real deal—an honest person who accepted the good and the bad about the Club. Since she was so open, I asked what she thought of Fred Rusk. Without the slightest hesitation, she rolled her eyes before saying that it takes all kinds, but that she could put up with him. After all, it's God's organization and Fred's the servant. Fred did the best he could, even if he was a bit flawed.

Helen and Connie became best of friends while we lived in New York City. Even when Connie learned about my doubts, she treated me with respect—not how most Club members would react. I appreciated that Helen had someone in whom to confide in this strange big city. She talked with Connie about everything. Sometimes I wondered if Connie was too good to be true, helping Helen and me during my transition.

Connie picked Helen up for the Thursday-night meeting and three hours later Helen was back home, radiating happiness. Everyone at the Hall liked her and she liked them. She had a short talk with Fred Rusk and explained why I wasn't at the meeting and that I had doubts about the Club. His response had put her in this good mood.

My reaction, it turned out, was normal for most young men leaving Bethel, at least for the first three months. Rusk called it

"Bethel Burnout." I had been on overload and needed to get my bearings. He said that I was one of the best young public speakers he had seen during his years at Bethel. In fact, he hoped I would deliver a special talk at the Thursday-night meeting in six weeks. He wanted Helen to give me his best wishes, and added, "Brother Kelly needs a little time off, a short vacation."

That conversation with Rusk had alleviated a lot of Helen's concerns about me not being a believer. But, his comments triggered two new questions: What did I have to do to make people believe that this religion wasn't for me? And "Bethel Burnout", what did that mean? I still had contacts at Bethel, and I knew that I could always count on Bert and Charley. Perhaps one of them could clue me in.

Bert & Charley
Chapter 5

During our first month in the City, I kept busy painting apartments while Helen attended meetings or spent time in the door-to-door ministry. Still, we found plenty of time to explore the City during our free time. We went to movies, walked the streets, picnicked in Central Park, enjoyed NYC's best museums, and attended day rehearsals at Radio City Music Hall. We also started putting marbles in a jar, a suggestion from Frank Kenner.

Frank was a Bethelite, but not a typical one. He had been invited to work at the Club's headquarters because of his painting and construction skills. I met him after he had been at Bethel for six months. A day after I told President Knorr I planned to leave Bethel, he knocked on my door and asked if we could talk.

He had come to Bethel from Illinois on the advice of his congregation servant. Frank had been a lukewarm JW and was told that if he worked and lived at Bethel, the lights would go on. His faith would be rejuvenated. Now he knew better. He saw that the Club was all smoke and mirrors. But he had squandered all of his savings to get to Bethel and now needed money to leave. He did not want to be homeless when he walked away.

I invited Frank to work with me on several painting projects before Helen and I were married. While we painted, Frank told me things I should and shouldn't do. A 32-year-old lifelong bachelor, he fancied himself a big-brother sage. Very late into a painting project, he recommended that I put a marble in a jar for every time Helen and I "Do It" after we get married. Then he told me that after a year, we should reverse the cycle, and start taking the marbles out of the jar. He bet me a six-pack of beer that we couldn't remove all the marbles, regardless of how long we were married.

Most of Frank's advice went in one ear and out the other. But this novel idea stuck. Two weeks into our marriage, I suggested to Helen that we put marbles in a jar, per Frank Kenner, although he would never know. And to my surprise, she agreed. I'm proud to say that Helen and I debunked Frank's theory, although it took us longer than I thought. But as we adjusted to married life and the variety of activities available to us, we didn't discuss religion and Helen never badgered me, not even once, to attend meetings.

One day, while Helen was in the door-to-door work with Connie, I took a subway to meet with Charley and Bert at their Brooklyn Heights apartment. I rang the doorbell and a husky guy answered the door. After introducing myself, he invited me in. Charley greeted me and said this guy was Stuart MacPherson, his little brother. I found that hard to believe, given his size. Stu had only been there a few days, but he was there to stay, now a full partner in Bert and Charley's building maintenance business. This partnership would also help Stu "get the Club monkey off his back," as Charley described it.

Stu grew up as a Club member in Big Rapids, Michigan, eighty miles northeast of Helen's childhood home. During his last year of high school, Stu wrote Charley, reporting he wanted out of the Club. Could his big brother help? Charley convinced Bert that Stu would be a good addition to their business. So after Stu graduated, he moved in with them. Now here with a good job, Stu had a means to leave his Club identity in Michigan. No one in the Club would be the wiser.

If a baptized Club member stops attending meetings or participating in the door-to-door work, they become a marked person. They will soon be visited by two elders, who will express interest in that person's spiritual well-being. The elders are really there to find out why the person left God's organization. To them, the only reason someone leaves is because he did something wrong. It could be sex out of wedlock, stealing, lying, or any one of many Club taboos.

According to Club theology, once a member commits a grievous sin, God's Holy Spirit abandons that person, allowing the Devil and his demons to take control. If the sinner confesses to his or her wrongdoing, the elders prescribe a long-term remedy. But Stu didn't want to go through that ordeal. If he told the elders that he wasn't a believer, they would assume him to be an apostate. If he didn't deny this assumption, he would be excommunicated and shunned. No social contact with family members would be allowed.

The Ghost of Separation Uses Shunning to Haunt Its Victims

So Stu chose to disappear. If someone wanted to know why he wasn't coming to meetings, his parents could say he left home to take a job in New York. That would end the conversation. This would terminate the elders' responsibility and allow Stu the anonymity he wanted. Charley said, "That's how you play the game, if you're smart."

When I asked Bert and Charley about Bethel Burnout, they told me it was quite common with young men leaving the Club's headquarters. They come to Bethel as naïve adult boys, but after a few years, they are fully aware of the double standards. They are also tired of the exhausting work and at some stage of questioning if God is truly the driving force behind the Club's success. So when they leave to go back home, they need time off. The reality of a long-time cult experience is similar to a drug addiction. While the young man may think he can quit cold turkey, it's easier said than done.

The Ghost of Separation Makes it Difficult to Bring Closure to One's JW Experience

When people have been taught all their lives that those who aren't Club members are not fit to associate with and that they are controlled by demons, that programming, that *misinformation*, isn't easily removed. However determined they may be to leave, they don't have a social structure in place to help them start their new life. Their family and friends are Club members—this is their community—and for better or for worse, the only community they've ever known. It's very difficult to leave unemotionally. While they aren't consciously aware of it, their comfort zone is still that community. That's not easy to change.

When a young man leaves Bethel, unless he is very unusual, he will not have read anything but Club publications. Secular knowledge is viewed as the Devil's workshop. While growing up, the Club did his thinking, and programmed him well. The young man leaving Bethel will find it very difficult to think on his own. This is one of the many ghosts he will have to face. So, while he may be in the early stages of challenging some of the Club's doctrines, he doesn't have an alternative. In other words, he does not know *what* he believes.

The Ghost of Inadequacy Makes it Difficult to Think for Its Victims

Mark Twain focused on this phenomenon in his essay "Corn-Pone Opinions." He refers to a person's religious beliefs, at any time during one's adult life, as "corn-pone opinions." He reasoned that "a person generally conforms to the majority view of his church by calculation and intention; that a cold thought-out and independent verdict about religion is a most rare thing—if indeed it ever exists. People are not trained to think when it comes to religion. They get their notions and habits and opinions from outside influences; they don't have to study them."

Why are Jehovah's Witnesses Jehovah's Witnesses? Twain believed that "very few people in the world have an opinion about religion which they acquired on their own. It came about through association and sympathies, not from reasoning and examination. Broadly speaking, there is nothing but corn-pone opinions. More specifically, corn-pone stands for self-approval."

Twain contends, "People think that they think about God, His grand plan, and what He requires of them, and they do; but they think with their church, not independently. They arrive at convictions, but they are drawn from a partial view of the matter at hand, which is of no particular value."

This is the mindset, whether the young man realizes it or not, when he leaves Bethel and decides to stop attending meetings or going in the door-to-door work. It's one of many ghosts—dysfunctional behavior patterns, bad information—he subconsciously acquired from the time he spent in the Club. Those ghosts will haunt and hamper his ability to leave. Soon, he begins to feel guilty and experiences a loss of self-approval.

Feeling Guilty and the Loss of Self-Approval

Where will he go to get affirmation that he is a good person and worthy of God's love? If his family belongs to the Club and he leaves, they will disown him. They will in effect quarantine him, treating him as if he has a contagious disease.

Shunning

Eventually, he will succumb and make a comeback. All is quickly forgiven. He had Bethel Burnout, but he's all better now.

While I appreciated the advice, one of the things that bothered me about Bert and Charley, and now Stu, related to the significant amounts of foul language they used. Everything was f-ing this, or mother-f-ing that. I wondered why they thought it necessary to incessantly use this kind of language. Did it have something to do with leaving the Club, or maybe repressed anger?

Before going home, Bert asked if Helen and I would like to join Charley and him on a long weekend drive back to west Michigan. They planned to visit Charley's parents in Big Rapids in August. They could drop us off Friday night in Holland, and pick us up Monday morning. I figured that Helen would love the trip, but reminded Bert that she was a lady. She wouldn't approve of his colorful language.

True to form, Bert responded with a litany of creative vulgarities. He put on a one-man comedy act, one of his best performances. As much as I hated to encourage him, I started laughing and it took a while before I could stop. When I did, I thought of Mama.

When Mama socialized with hard-core Club members like Helen's mom, she tried to give the impression that all dirty jokes were disgusting. But if she happened to hear a well-told racy story from a more tolerant JW, she could go into a laughing fit. I found that funnier than the joke. Mama was not alone. Many Club members enjoyed hearing or telling dirty stories, vicariously acting out their suppressed beliefs about politics, movies, or sex. Yet, with other hard-core JWs, they'd condemn this kind of behavior as evil. The irony is that the God they claim to worship—Who sees everything and Who judges them on Judgment Day—appears to ignore what flesh-and-blood JWs can see and hear.

When I arrived home, Helen busied herself preparing dinner, but stopped to tell me about Robert Seekman and Frank Boss. "These guys are really interesting. They want to meet you. And they're studying the Bible with a Bethelite you know, Chuck Ambrose." That name got my attention.

Chuck, assigned to Helen's Hall, had once been labeled an SR—an acronym for a self-righteous Bethelite. You didn't complain about Bethel life to an SR. They tattled. But that ended when Chuck cut off his left hand in a printing press accident. Who knows how it happened, but after the accident the Club's president, Nathan Knorr, singled out Chuck during one of his infamous breakfast speeches, calling Chuck careless, irresponsible, and mindless. To make matters worse, Chuck sat trembling through the breakfast bashing, taking this needless rant as if guilty as charged.

To add insult to injury, the Club's doctor fitted Chuck with a cheap, light-purple rubber prosthesis. Anyone with a pinch of self-esteem wouldn't wear it to a Halloween party. While I had never met Chuck, I had seen him and his hand several times. Now it struck me as bizarre that Chuck Ambrose would still be a true-blue believer trying to convert these two guys Helen wanted me to meet.

Several days later, I met Robert and Frank at their apartment, a block from our house. Frank, a street-smart African-American Queen, had been off drugs for three months. Robert, half Frank's age, was pale white and refreshingly naïve, and had not been smoking peyote for three months. They had been studying the Bible—a structured six-month Club indoctrination process—with Chuck. They were far enough in their study that they planned to break up as partners, having just learned from Club literature that homosexuality was evil in the sight of God.

Frank had second thoughts and now mulled over this Club truth. Robert appeared excited about the prospect of getting on God's good side. They were both pleased to meet me. Frank, who liked to talk, shared their fascinating personal history. As I listened, I reflected on how the Club could be helpful at times. Both of these guys had been hardcore drug addicts, and this very structured high-control religion had given them the incentive to stop drugs, at least for the time being.

However, I wondered how the Club arrived at its homosexual spin. JWs are taught it's a choice that a person makes. While at Bethel, I worked with a young man who knew of his attraction to men, but he had practiced abstinence just like me, a heterosexual. So I figured that a person is born with a predisposition for a same-sex relationship. But with Frank and Robert, it appeared to be a non-issue. Drugs would have eventually killed them. With help from Chuck, these guys had found a way to beat this addiction, albeit with a less harmful addiction—a high-control religious experience.

A month passed and I hadn't attended a meeting or spent time in the door-to-door work. Then Helen informed me that Fred Rusk wanted to talk with me; he hoped we could talk at the next Sunday meeting. The request took me by surprise, as did my reaction of a nervous stomach and jangled nerves.

I had been so confident when I met with the president of the Club. I had no problem telling him about leaving Bethel. If he had allowed me, I'd have told him my plans to leave the Club as well. I realized this was not well thought out, given the problems *that* would have created in my relationship with Helen. In fact, I was pleased that President Knorr had stopped me from putting my foot into my mouth. Still, why did the thought of meeting with Rusk make me feel so uneasy?

The more I thought about it, going to the meeting wasn't the problem. I could do that. It was the talk! Helen had said a month before that Rusk wanted me to deliver a special talk at a Thursday night meeting. Standing on stage, dressed in my go-to-meeting clothes telling people stuff I didn't believe—outright lies—for fifteen minutes. Could I do that again? And why did Rusk want *me* to give the talk?

The Compromise
Chapter 6

Surprisingly, getting ready to go to the meeting was easy. Once inside the Hall, fifteen minutes early, I felt strangely comfortable and relaxed, like going to visit with old friends. The familial chatter that goes on in a Kingdom Hall before the meeting gets started was native white noise from my past sixteen years.

Several Bethelites I knew playfully greeted me. Connie treated me with a big hug. Robert shook my hand vigorously, like a long-lost friend. He looked so out of place with his former partner, Frank, conspicuously absent. Fred Rusk welcomed me, calling me Brother Kelly. He apologized that we couldn't visit longer. We would meet one-on-one after the second meeting. I met Chuck Ambrose for the first time, and while shaking his right hand, I gracelessly gawked at his other hand jiggling.

Helen introduced me to several of her friends, calling each one of them *Sister Mary, Sister Jones, etc*. They all appeared to be normal, non-fanatic-type Club members, except for one older Japanese lady with an odd air. After the introduction, she quickly turned around as if someone tapped her on the back. All blank space, but she greeted it like she did me. Could she be talking to an invisible person?

The first one-hour meeting on Sunday afternoon is called the Public Talk, its subject and content predetermined by Club hierarchy. Delivered by someone with a penis, the speaker had specific learning objectives to meet and Bible verses to read. He could salt and pepper his sermon with a few anecdotes, but they must come from recent issues of *The Watchtower* or other Club literature. Critical thinking skills played no role in the preparation of his speech.

Fortunately, Fred Rusk delivered the sermon that day. While he had a monotone speaking style, his research skills cleverly masked it. He shared interesting bits of Club trivia that I hadn't heard before. Still, after thirty minutes, my mind began to wander.

I saw Chuck Ambrose's deformed rubber hand dangling in the aisle, upsetting me all over again. He appeared happy and oblivious to his affliction, listening intently to what he must have heard hundreds of times before. Oddly enough, Chuck fit in this community.

I watched Helen enthusiastically look up and read Bible verses that Fred referred to, captivated by his talk. Unlike me, she had not been coerced to attend. She wanted to be here. These were her people. The talk energized her.

Robert Seekman looked like a plump boy happily gorging himself on spiritual food in God's kitchen. As silly as this stuff sounded to me, Robert excitedly listened, seeming to believe everything Fred said. I surmised that this was Robert's Theocratic halfway house, where he felt safe and loved.

"Different strokes for different folks," I thought. For a moment, I wondered about the harmlessness of this addiction, this need that some people have to believe an unusual spin on world events, the nature of God, and His grand plan—and to listen to the same message over and over again. That is, until I observed one of the children in attendance. The little girl had been well-mannered for forty-five minutes when she started to act up. Her father's harsh, audible response, "If you don't stop that, I'm going to take you outside and spank you," brought me back to reality.

It seemed wrong to me to force children to sit through a bunch of mumbo jumbo they don't understand. Yet the Club persistently tells members that the Bible admonishes them to bring their babies and small children to all five of its weekly meetings. To make matters worse, spanking is considered an act of tough love. It is done at Kingdom Halls all around the world. I witnessed the father taking his daughter outside the Hall and spanking her. I cringed when I heard the girl screaming. Many people would have considered it child abuse. But that's not how Club members see it.

After the Public Talk, we took a fifteen-minute break. When Helen and I went outside to get a breath of fresh air, I told her how idiotic I found the Club's policy with respect to disciplining children at meetings. That off my chest, we visited with two of her new friends. Then we went back into the Hall for the second one-hour meeting, The Watchtower Study.

In this meeting, *The Watchtower* (WT) is used. It's the Club's official house organ and a magazine first printed in 1879. Each week, in a question-and-answer format, a specific article in the WT is reviewed. Members are advised to underline the answers to the questions on the bottom of the page before coming to the meeting. A man, the Watchtower Study Servant, presides. He asks the questions designated for a specific paragraph, attendees raise their hands to answer, he picks someone from the audience, and a microphone is passed to the answerer. Generally, there's enough information in each paragraph for three or four comments from different people, ultimately paraphrasing everything in print. When no more hands are raised, the WT Servant asks the person on stage with him to read the paragraph. Then he proceeds to the next paragraph.

Underlining Answers to Questions in *The Watchtower*

This quintessential learning-by-rote exercise is the most boring of the five Club meetings, at least for the uninvolved. In other words, the Watchtower Study Meeting—a third-grade-level, find-the-answer game—is a big-time bore to anyone who doesn't participate. Thinking skills are not needed. Attendees find the answer. If they are so moved, they raise their hands like school children. Most attendees appear excited to have the opportunity to recite the answer out loud. I noticed how Helen's energy level rose from the experience, her participation in the process was the key.

The Watchtower Study Meeting is also a significant incubator for the ghosts that people acquire from their JW experience. No one is allowed to ask questions or challenge the answers during the meeting. Club members are advised to underline all the answers the previous day. The act of verbally sharing misinformation into a microphone to a hundred other believers further validates information that ain't so.

The Ghost of Misinformation

How do I know that it ain't so? When at Bethel in 1964, I went to the Club's library and read several copies of *The Watchtower* printed in the 1920s and 1930s. The massive amounts of misinformation printed in those issues were obvious in 1964, even to the most hardcore Club member. One blatant ain't so predicted Armageddon would occur in 1925, coming directly from the Club's president. When he issued his revelation, *Watchtower* readers believed it was the truth. I personally found it disturbing. But most JWs don't see it that way. Why? Because they believe God constantly sheds new light, new truths, from *The Watchtower*. But then again, that's Club spin. Which of course begs the question: *What truth is currently being taught that will be misinformation thirty to forty years from now?*

At the WT Study Meeting, I noticed that the Japanese lady raised her hand incessantly. However, the Watchtower Servant didn't call on her to answer a question. Helen told me later that she had some kind of a mental disorder. Had she been asked to answer a question, she would have responded with some silly comment unrelated to the question. This tickled me as I thought that the questions asked in *The Watchtower* were silly anyway, unrelated to reality. So why were adults attracted to this religion? Could it be related to some kind of mental disorder?

After the meeting, Helen decided she would go home with Connie and start working on an early supper. We didn't know how long my conversation with Fred would last. In fact, I waited twenty minutes before he asked me to follow him to a private room off the main auditorium.

Once in the room, he apologized for the delay, poured coffee and asked me to take a seat. He came right to the point. "Brother Kelly, it was nice to see you at the Hall today and your wife, Sister Kelly, is a good addition to the congregation. Everyone likes her."

Fred didn't use the words Bethel Burnout, but I knew that's what he alluded to when he said, "I want you to know that I understand what's happening in your life right now. It's not unusual for young hardworking ex-Bethelites to do what you're doing."

Not sure what he knew about me or what Helen had told him, I decided to set the record straight and interrupted. "Fred, I want you to know that I have my doubts about many Club beliefs. I felt this way long before I came to Bethel. I also don't like going in the door-to-door work."

"Listen, Brother Kelly. You don't have to explain a thing. I understand. Between you and me, you aren't the only one who finds it demeaning to knock on the doors of strangers. President Knorr hasn't spent time in the door-to-door work for years. There are plenty of other ways to serve Jehovah. Your excellent record at Bethel speaks for itself. You are a good public speaker. Brother Ambrose tells me that you're doing a great job helping the ex-drug addicts. And, I think it's good that your wife enjoys spending time in the door-to-door ministry. I just approved her vacation pioneer application for June."

He continued, saying, "If you think you're the only one who has doubts from time to time, you are very naïve. We all have them. How can you not when you've lived at Bethel? The apostles had them. Paul had them. Why, even Jesus questioned if God had forsaken him during the last hour of his life. An occasional doubt is normal. But you've come too far to give up now. Give yourself some time and you'll see everything clearly."

Flabbergasted, I could also see that Fred wanted to end this conversation. On a specific mission, he quickly changed the subject and said, "So Brother Kelly, we have a special talk coming up on the Service Meeting—a talk that I'd like you to give. I have the outline here and I think you'll do a good job." Then he handed it to me.

I reached out and grabbed it, a spontaneous reflex. I should have waited. It would have bought time to engage Rusk in some clarification about "doubts" and me helping two ex-drug addicts. What did he think I was doing with Robert and Frank? While I knew them well, I had never talked religion. But I had missed my opportunity, and with the talk outline in hand, I decided to read it.

The essence of the fifteen-minute talk answered the question, How could a person ultimately know which religious group followed Jesus Christ? According to the outline, if the group truly shows love between one another, stop the search and get on board. The lead scripture for the sermon, John 13: 34, 35, read, "I am giving you a new commandment, that you love one another. By this all, you will know that you are my disciples, if you have love among yourselves."

In a nutshell, if a sincere, honest person is interested in finding the organization, the one and only group which God's Holy Spirit directs, it would be easy. All she or he would need to do is find a religious group drenched in love, and bingo, they just found it. The assumption was that only Jehovah's Witnesses exhibit that kind of love. The outline listed other Bible verses that would have to be used. By the time I finished reading the talk's learning objectives, I knew I could deliver the message. But, I would do it my way and have some fun as well. So I agreed to give the talk. We shook hands and the meeting was over.

I had a strange feeling as I walked to my car, second thoughts about what I planned to do. I might get myself in trouble. After the short drive to our apartment, I found it difficult to find a parking space. New York City has an alternate parking ordinance six days of the week. This allows for an open lane and easy access for morning trash pickup. I circled our block and nearby blocks for nearly fifteen minutes before I found a place. By this time, I knew exactly what I would say, certain that I had done the right thing.

After living and working in New York City for a month, I knew where I didn't want to spend the bulk of my married life. When Helen and I had children, I did not want to raise them in the concrete jungle of NYC, nor did I want to be a building superintendent and a handyman all my life. Unfortunately, I didn't know what I wanted to do or where I wanted to live. I ruled out Nebraska as Mama lived there. I also didn't want to move to west Michigan because of the proximity to Helen's mother.

But I hadn't confided these sentiments to Helen. Happy with her life, she thoroughly enjoyed the big city and her new friends. And our marriage couldn't have been better. It also didn't hurt that both of us embraced a frugal lifestyle, to make and save as much money as we could.

For me, when opportunity knocked for the right change of scenery, I wanted to be ready. Money problems would not stop us. Still, I was aware that I couldn't open the door of opportunity by myself. While I could wait for the right person or circumstance to come along, patience went AWOL at an early age in my DNA. So I made a big decision. I needed help from a community, a community that only a few months ago I planned to abandon.

My conversation with Fred Rusk confirmed what now stirred in my mind: not all Club members were as strict and severe as Mama. Many had well-paying jobs with secular connections that I needed. If I wanted to find a challenging, well-paying job in a part of the country I liked, I needed help from the only community that I had connections to, the Club community.

This Bethel Burnout stuff worked in my favor. As Charley

explained, I needed to be smart about how I played the game and made my exit. Being both an ex-Bethelite in good standing with the Club and being honest with myself could be possible, an asset that I must not waste.

For four months, May thru August, I occasionally attended meetings with Helen. I also delivered the Fred Rusk sponsored talk. I turned in creative time slips at the Hall so I wouldn't be considered inactive. Helen and I took a short vacation to Holland, Michigan with the help of Bert and Charley. I waited for an opportunity that didn't materialize. And yes, all of this needs some immediate explanation.

My fifteen-minute sermon turned out to be a big success, at least from my point of view. I rallied my semi-bombastic convention voice for the talk, pontificating about the pervasive love at Bethel. I asserted that, starting at the top with the Club's president down to the general rank-and-file, Bethelite love doesn't get better. No gossip or friction existed among members at Kingdom Halls around the world—just love and kindness. I performed a Monty Python spoof in a Kingdom Hall.

In reality, Knorr and Franz were cold and heartless men. To get ahead at Bethel, random acts of kindness wouldn't cut it. Gossip and intense rivalries were commonplace at Bethel and in all the Halls I ever attended. I thought that someone in the audience would have caught on that it was a joke, a parody. But when people are not trained to think, it's difficult to see such a thing.

With only a few minutes to go, I thought I had pulled it off. But, suddenly, Fred stood up and walked briskly to the back of the Hall. Certain that only I could see him, he sliced a finger across his neck. But I had two minutes to go. It would have been awkward to stop. Again, he signaled me. This time he didn't seem to care who noticed. Fortunately, I had only fifteen seconds to go. To Fred, it must have seemed an eternity.

After the meeting, I walked toward the back door with Helen. But before we could leave, Fred asked to speak with me. I followed him to the vacated magazine counter, where he abruptly whirled around and grabbed me by my shirt collar. He yanked it several times and sternly said, "When I tell you to leave the stage, you are to leave it immediately! Do you understand?" I nodded my flushed face and walked away. It was the last talk I would ever give at a Kingdom Hall.

Our mini-vacation, chauffeured by Bert and Charley in August, turned out to be an eye-opener and a nice break from the City. The dynamics between Helen and Bert during the ride to Holland could not have been better. Charley did most of the driving, while Bert entertained us with his off-color stories and jokes. We shared lots of laughs and Helen took no offense over the constant use of the f-word as an adjective, adverb, noun and interjection. However, by drop-off time late Friday, we were ready for a change in company, although not prepared to go from one extreme to the other.

We were greeted by Helen's mother, Gertrude, and Helen's sister, Esther. Helen's dad, employed by the Holland Power Plant, worked the second shift, so we didn't see him until the next day. From the moment we walked into the house until we left Monday morning, Gertrude treated me like a ranking officer in the Club hierarchy. She had no idea that I hadn't been in the door-to-door work for over five months. She assumed that I held a leading role at the West Manhattan congregation we attended. Neither Helen nor I told her otherwise.

We hadn't been there an hour when Gertrude told us about a heavy-duty mission she had been planning for months. She intended to work a fail-proof plan to convert and save Helen's older sister, Ellie, her two brothers, Hannity and Harris, and her father. Convinced that Armageddon could come any day, two years at the most, it seemed that Gertrude didn't want it on her conscience that they may be destroyed along with other nonbelievers. They needed to be in the Truth now. I silently convulsed at the spitting image of Mama before me, and what made it even more pathetic— Gertrude figured I could help with the conversions.

Gertrude thought that Helen's twin brother, Harris, a very likeable, mild-mannered man, would be the easiest to convert. Ten months before, when Harris told his mother that his wedding would take place in a Lutheran church, she did not like it. She tried to change his mind, but to no avail. Most Club members won't go inside a church, believing the Devil and his demons control all religions except theirs. Club members think that unseen evil spirits haunt all false church sanctuaries. If they go inside and stay too long, they will inevitably lose God's good grace.

Gertrude knew that Helen and I planned to visit with Harris and his wife, Jane, the following day. She wanted me to explain the JW spin on God's grand plan, a concept they could not yet grasp. Both Helen and I were tired by this time. Not just from our long day in the car, but from this long one-sided conversation. So we said that we needed to get some sleep.

Helen and I met Harris and Jane at their trailer the next day. What piqued my interest had nothing to do with religion. We didn't discuss that. It had to do with Jane's father, Walter. I had heard about this giant from Big Rapids, Michigan before. At six-foot-seven inches and 300 pounds, he played the nasty villain role in one of Charley's cherished stories about a son-of-a-bitch that he planned to get some day.

I hadn't known Charley a week at Bethel when he favored me with a tale about this monster of a man, the fire chief for Big Rapids. Charley met the guy in the door-to-door work. They started a conversation and all went well until Charley pulled out a copy of *The Watchtower* and *Awake*. Aware that Charley was a JW, Walter went into a tirade about him not saluting the flag, fighting for his country, and more. He demanded that Charley get off his property and never return. Charley didn't like taking orders from anyone and stalled. This infuriated Walter. So he physically touched and pushed Charley in an effort to help him leave. That's when Charley went berserk. Railing his arms in all directions, he machine-gunned the man with the f-word. As I recall Charley's exact words, "I think I set a world record for the amount of times one person was told to go fuck himself." So unlike a good JW in the door-to-door work, but so like Charley when provoked.

Irony doesn't get any better than learning that Walter's daughter was my sister-in-law. I couldn't wait to tell Charley the full story during our drive back to New York City. My thoughts also went to wondering what Walter would do if he knew what Gertrude was scheming for his daughter.

On Sunday, we went to the small Kingdom Hall that Helen once attended. What a contrast from the big congregation and Hall in New York City. While there, I took the opportunity to talk with Dan Dykstra. He had been the master of ceremonies at our wedding reception but I had little opportunity to get to know him. An engaging man with a great sense of humor, he never once talked religion, which I liked. Employed by a large metal boat manufacturer, Roamer Yachts, Dan told me that if Helen and I moved to west Michigan he thought I could get a job with Roamer.

After the meeting, Gertrude shared some bad news about an 85-year-old brother who had been a Club member for years. Present at the meeting we attended, he had just become inactive. In other words, during the last six months, he stopped participating in the door-to-door work, no longer turning in a monthly time slip—a preprinted form dropped into a special box at the Hall every month, reporting hours and literature placed. Not a good sign. The man had likely lost his faith, which is a common phobia for most Club members. Gertrude spent a lot of time telling us a lot about nothing.

However, as she related the story, I wondered what she would have thought of me and my duplicity. While I had stopped going in the door-to-door work, I turned in creative time slips each month for the few hours I spent with Robert and Frank, although we did not discuss religion. I didn't want to go on the inactive list as it could hurt my chances if a good job opportunity turned up in the Club community.

When we arrived back at our New York City apartment, it felt good to be home. There's no way that I could live in the same house with Helen's mother, definitely Mama's clone. Holding my tongue had been a challenge. I could have easily blown my cover had we stayed longer. It also helped me appreciate Helen. While still a believer, she allowed me to do my thing and never complained.

In September, I went on a painting frenzy. Tim helped on a number of jobs and I heard firsthand about his progress with Esther. My friend, Frank Kenner, helped as well. A good worker, a skilled painter, he was another ear into which I could talk honestly about the Club. He planned to leave Bethel, and he, like Charley, knew how to play the game and provided me with many good ideas.

As September came to a close, I had saved $4,000 dollars.

However, the big opportunity to get us out of NYC had not yet knocked at our door. But that would change in a very dramatic way.

Opportunity Knocks
Chapter 7

Our most dangerous experience in New York City occurred while Helen and I were taking a walk, approaching the corner of West 70th Street and Amsterdam, near Needle Park. We heard a loud boom, like a bomb exploding. We stopped and looked around. Within seconds we saw several policemen with guns drawn running toward a large bank building. Helen said, "Let's follow them!" I looked at her in disbelief, grabbed her hand, and said it wouldn't be a good idea. Stray bullets were as lethal as those intended to harm someone. We never found out what happened, guessing that thieves must have targeted a bank vault.

While we lived in the City, we observed many forms of lawlessness—domestic violence, gang fights, solicitation by prostitutes, verbal threats from a tenant, and road rage. Yet, I never felt like Helen and I were in personal danger. We avoided problems. When a policeman asked for a cash donation, I told him how much I appreciated his hard work, but he would have to talk with the owner of the building.

Helen and I had become good friends with Robert Seekman. Clean from his drug addiction, he was an interesting, resourceful young man. The Club's heavy-duty structure and control had helped. Not yet a religious fanatic, Robert easily accepted me and we talked freely about a variety of subjects. He helped me with odd jobs and joined Helen when she needed someone to go with her in the door-to-door work.

Robert and Frank made a clean break in their relationship when Frank decided Club rules didn't fit his lifestyle. He stopped his studies with Chuck Ambrose and found a new partner. I talked with him several times after that and he seemed pleased that Robert had found a purpose for his life. He told me, "It works for him, but not for me."

Helen *vacation pioneered*— 75 hours of door-to-door work per month— for two months while we lived in the City and it didn't interfere with our time together. In fact, it gave her something to do while I worked. It also provided an opportunity to rub shoulders with some unusual people, which the Club often attracts. One of them was the older mentally-challenged Japanese lady. A recent convert, she had a unique way of introducing herself to people in the door-to-door ministry. She would knock on a door and wait. If the homeowner inquired, "Who's there?" She would tell them that it's an angel. Helen tried to get her to change, but she had a mind of her own, convinced that God protected each person in the door-to-door work with a personal angel.

In October, Helen missed her period and thought she might be pregnant. We talked with Connie, who knew of a doctor, albeit a little old, who would see Helen right away, and he confirmed her pregnancy.

I had a premonition the month before that we had conceived a baby. When Helen told me she had a normal period, I had mixed emotions. Definitely dysfunctional thinking on my part, as I had no idea where we would move and what I'd do for a living.

So now we knew Helen was pregnant, thinking the baby would come sometime the first week of June 1965. Fortunately, Helen, like me, didn't want to raise our child in New York City. We wanted to live outside a big city, in a residential area where I could find work. And we agreed that living near our parents, be it Nebraska or west Michigan, was not a good idea. So where would we go?

I talked with several people in Helen's congregation and Bethelites. But no one knew who could help me find a good job. By the end of the year, we had no leads. Not until March 1965 did Frank Kenner tell me about a landscaper located fifty miles south of Chicago. He was expanding his business and needed additional workers, willing to invest in the training needed for the right person. The only catch was that he had strongly encouraged Frank to go to Bethel; so he may be a gung-ho believer. Still, I called and we talked for thirty minutes. Impressed with my Bethel experience, he offered me an entry-level position. It had potential if I had what it takes.

This valid job offer would get us out of the City. The downside: I might be working for a hard-core JW. If so, he wouldn't be pleased when he found out that I was a nonbeliever. Perhaps I could play the game for several months. If I liked landscaping, I could quit and find another employer.

I wanted a second option. So I called Dan Dykstra to see if the company he worked for was hiring. I felt some trepidation, knowing it would mean moving near Helen's mother. Pleased that I called, Dan informed me of an immediate opening for an experienced painter. He had worked at Roamer Yachts in Holland, Michigan, for over a year and liked his work. He said that I should give the company a call.

When I talked with the Personnel Director, I learned I had the job if I could pass the physical and that the starting pay rate was much higher than what the Illinois landscaper offered. The company knew all about me. Dan had told them about my painting experience and that my wife grew up in Holland.

Helen and I were discussing the pros and cons of both job offers when I received a call from Dan. He told me about an attractive two-bedroom apartment in Hamilton, Michigan. It didn't require a lease and we could move in the last week in April, paying rent at $60 a month. I thanked him for the call and said I'd get back to him.

It would be nice to be near family when the baby came. Helen would also be happy in Illinois, if that's what I decided. The job there appeared to have better long-term potential. The only catch was that I would be working for a Club member. Yes, Helen's mother lived in west Michigan. But then, Helen had a nonbelieving father and three nonbelieving siblings in the area. So I accepted the job in Holland an hour later and asked Dan to make the deposit on our apartment.

Our plans were to leave New York City toward the end of April. Shortly after we arrived in Holland, I would take my physical. If all went well, I would start my new job right away. By the first week in June, we would be a family of three. If the baby was a boy, his name would be Keith Evans Kelly and if a girl, we would call her Kimberly Sue Kelly.

However, we had no idea that misinformation might jeopardize those plans. And the Club wouldn't be the guilty party on this one. Helen's New York City doctor, in the twilight of his practice, had miscalculated the conception date. We had no idea of the complications this would create when the baby arrived.

Okay, the Club Doesn't Have a Monopoly on Misinformation

Our First Year in West Michigan
Chapter 8

Our departure from New York City was bittersweet. Helen and I had lived there for over a year and it couldn't have been a better place to start a marriage. I learned more about her during that time than any similar period over the next forty-seven years. Our marriage survived my openness and partial dissociation with the Club. We saved money. And, in NYC we conceived our first child. But we were ready for the move.

We knew that our new, sight-unseen apartment in Hamilton would be larger than our bunker in the City. But we had no idea it would be a palace in comparison. It was five times the size, with a mammoth stove and refrigerator, and lots of closet space. A spacious wooded area nearby gave it the appearance of an up-scale motel complex planted in the lush countryside. When our furniture arrived, we were again reminded of how little living space we had had in the City.

Helen, more tired than usual, blamed it on the move, the excitement and the work needed to turn a house into a home. After a week, she thought she should see a doctor. I called her older sister, Ellie, and she made the appointment for May 4. Helen was in the doctor's office for a long time before she walked out crying and dilating. The baby could come at any moment. We had to go to the hospital immediately.

In hindsight, we were very naïve and very fortunate. We later learned that the conception took place in August. To add insult to injury, Helen's New York City doctor had not only failed to get the date right, he hadn't prepared her for childbirth. It would be a difficult birth.

For over twenty-four hours of labor, Helen struggled and resisted bringing the baby into the world. Several times she informed me that it would be an only child, and future sex was out of the question. But as hard as she fought, she made progress. Finally, a nurse escorted me to the reception area while another wheeled Helen by gurney to the birthing room. I waited for several nervous hours before the doctor appeared with a big smile. "You have a healthy baby boy, Mr. Kelly, and his mother is doing well, considering the ordeal she's been through."

"When can I see my son?" I anxiously inquired.

"I'll have a nurse bring him out after he's cleaned up."

Several minutes later a nurse appeared, cradling my little baby boy. A miracle! Directly in front of me lay Keith Evans Kelly, a beautiful, vibrant baby, even if his eyes were tightly closed. A moment in time I will never forget. I wanted to hold him, to physically connect. But, the nurse's body language signaled that it wouldn't happen, at least not yet. Tired and at a loss for words, I suddenly noticed that Keith had a long bright-red mark branded on his forehead. So I anxiously asked, "What's that?"

Like any new parent, I wanted a healthy child who would grow up to be an intelligent, productive adult. My younger sister Susan, born with a permanent brain injury, could never leave home because of her birth defect. So when I noticed the mark, I wondered if Keith too might have a brain disorder. Needless to say, I was relieved to hear the nurse say, "Oh, that's a birth mark. Don't worry. It'll go away when he's older."

I went home feeling empty and strange without Helen. I had not slept alone for over a year. I called Ellie and asked if she would help me buy baby clothes and a bassinette. Everything had happened so quickly. I then broke down crying, a combination of tears of joy and frustration. I had this new person in my life but I felt disconnected from his arrival. I have revisited those emotions many times over the years, thinking how special it would have been to be in the delivery room when Keith was born. But in those days, it didn't happen.

Alone and unable to sleep, I thought about how I wanted to raise my little boy. I did not want him to grow up a Jehovah's Witness, that was for sure. But what should I teach him? Is there life after death? Did God position Himself as someone who needs to be worshipped and appeased like Jehovah's Witnesses believe? Is the Bible the inspired word of God?

I thought about how lucky we were that Keith didn't come into this world on our drive from New York City to Michigan. How ignorant and naïve could I be? But I would learn. I wanted to be a good father, the kind of father that I'd been deprived of.

I also thought about Helen's religious beliefs. While I believed they weren't true, I hadn't convinced her that I was right. And it definitely didn't help that I couldn't articulate my own beliefs about God and the Bible.

The Ghost of Inadequacy Makes it Difficult to Articulate Well-Thought-Out Beliefs

Pointing out discrepancies in the Club's interpretations of the Bible wasn't going to work. Yes, I had read the Bible from cover to cover several times, but I had difficulty finding a loving God or a roadmap for everlasting life in its pages.

However, bringing Helen and Keith home for the first time helped me reflect on what I did have. Mama had told me many times that the world would be destroyed at Armageddon before I reached the age of twenty. My fantasy had always been to have sex at least once, knowing I couldn't measure up to the Club's survival standards. Now twenty-one years old with a wife and baby, I felt good to be alive. If Mama had been right, I would have been dead along with all the other nonbelievers.

But reality quickly trumped my smugness. From that very first night at home, and for the next ninety days, Keith suffered from a severe case of colic. This combined with our inexperience as parents made the next three months more than challenging.

Fortunately, I enjoyed my work at Roamer Yachts. While I seldom attended meetings and no longer went in the door-to-door work, Keith and I accompanied Helen at social events hosted by Club members. Helen's mom, my Roamer workmates, and other JWs always treated me well, acting as if I suffered from Bethel Burnout and would soon see the light.

Several months into my job at Roamer, I told Helen that I didn't want to be a painter for the rest of my life. I wanted to go to college and develop skills denied me by Mama's Club beliefs. But to make this possible, we would have to move to Grand Rapids.

In June, I saw an ad for an apartment management position in Wyoming, a suburb of Grand Rapids. It required a qualified married couple to rent and maintain three eight-family buildings, the Colrain Apartments. The pay: free rent and utilities for a large one-bedroom apartment.

I mailed our application and received a favorable response. The owner of the Colrain Apartments, Mr. Leo, had talked with our NYC landlord, Mr. Kay, and Kay raved about our credentials. Leo wanted to meet in his office and asked us to bring Keith. I dressed in a suit and tie, which did not go unnoticed. Leo offered us the job, and insisted that he personally show us the new apartments before we made our decision.

The first eight-family building was nearly complete. Builders were framing two additional buildings. They would be ready for occupancy at year's end. Leo walked with us to the back side of the second floor, showing us the two-bedroom unit. Then he opened the door to what could be our one-bedroom apartment. Helen couldn't hide her excitement for the big, never-been-lived-in apartment with its large refrigerator/freezer, stove and thick green carpet. Before leaving, we agreed to take the job, starting in July.

Two weeks before we moved, my brother Tim and Helen's sister Esther were married in Holland, with Helen as the maid of honor and me as the best man. Tim had left Bethel per plan, but he didn't have the financial means to pioneer. So he applied for a job and was hired at Roamer Yachts.

One thing I have learned over the years is encapsulated in the saying, *"You aren't critically aware of what you believe, until you have children."* And so it was for Helen and me, but we were going in different directions.

After Helen and I moved to the Colrain Apartments, she attended all the Club's five weekly meetings and spent twenty hours a month in the door-to-door work. For the first time, she expressed a mild sense of urgency to prepare for Armageddon's imminent arrival. Helen didn't want her new son to die during the holocaust.

Your Son Keith is Going to Die at Armageddon Unless…

When she asked me to attend meetings, I occasionally joined her, but I refused to go door-to-door. Finally, in September of 1965 I told her that I would not go to any more meetings. I wasn't a believer. But, I wouldn't stop her. If that's what she wanted, I'd help her as much as I could. When she asked what she should tell people at the Kingdom Hall, I told her that I would write a letter of dissociation.

A few days after sending my resignation notice, I received a telephone call from the circuit servant. This man was a traveling minister from the Club's headquarters who had the authority to appoint and remove elders for the Kingdom Hall. He said he had a copy of my resignation, but not to worry. He had some good news for me. When and where could we meet?

At our meeting, he took out my resignation letter and ripped it up, saying my impulse to dissociate was a symptom of Bethel Burnout, that I needed to get back into the swing of things, and that as a natural leader, I needed more responsibilities. He then pulled out a letter from headquarters appointing me as the Assistant Congregation Servant. He didn't have a snippet of doubt that the appointment would change my mind. It never occurred to him that I could be a nonbeliever, unwilling to sacrifice my life for a religious fantasy.

While I can't be certain, I think someone who knew me at Bethel thought I'd be swayed with power. I often saw Club members tempted by the love of power—definitely not the power of love—at Bethel. Once people give in to this form of temptation, it changes them. The elixir of power corrupts. After a person tastes it, it's almost impossible to turn back.

When the circuit servant made his offer, I sat stunned. It was not what I expected. He no doubt misinterpreted my momentary lapse of words. However, I would not change my mind and told him so. Perhaps someday I would have a change of heart, but for the moment my decision would stand. He looked shocked and bewildered. Difficult for a sincere believer, a genuinely nice guy (which he was), to understand, but we parted on good terms and no witch-hunting followed. That is *not* how it would have played out today, which will be explained later in the book.

After officially dissociating myself from the Club in the fall of 1965, finding a better job became my top priority. I interviewed with The Grand Rapids Employer's Association and took two aptitude tests. A day later, I learned that my test results weren't the norm at this small employment agency. The interviewer couldn't figure out why I wasn't going to college and said, "You would make an excellent accountant." He encouraged me to take night classes at Davenport College right away. If a job opened up that fit my qualifications, he would call me. Toward the end of October, I received that call. Impressed with my test results, an old-line manufacturer in the northwest part of the city wanted to interview me.

Dressed in my go-to-meeting clothes—a suit, white shirt and

tie—I entered the dreary factory office of a company in its decline. The place had not been painted for years and this should have been a red flag. The interviewer asked lots of questions, many that didn't make sense to me. Fortunately, he seemed to like my answers. I did so well that he asked me to take a physical the same day. Two hours later, I brought back a good report from the doctor and he offered me the job. I could start anytime. I wanted the job, but said that I needed to give my current employer, Roamer Yachts, two weeks' notice.

What I didn't tell him was that I also wanted to make a trip to Nebraska. I needed to tell Mama in person that I had dissociated myself from the Club. And I had no idea how she would react.

.

The Bible Gets in Their Way
Chapter 9

I knew that what I had to say wouldn't change Mama's beliefs. She's never allowed facts to get in the way of her strong convictions. She, like most people who believe they've found the truth, stop searching for it. *She believes what she wants to believe.* Her religious beliefs are personal, permanent and always right. But she needed to hear directly from me that I had left the Club. As long as I didn't tell her that I had become a Catholic, Methodist or an atheist, she would think there was still some hope for me. She wouldn't disown me, not yet.

My wish today, although it wouldn't have swayed her, is that I knew then what many reputable seminaries were teaching students about the Bible. In particular, the well-documented history of who wrote, edited, organized, marketed and preserved it, and when and why they did it. But what I did know was that most Christians didn't read the Bible the way one would expect of a cherished book. Yet they passionately believe that it's the inerrant, sacred Word of God. Why? Because it is! That's what their parents believed or someone at their church said. To me, that is not a responsible response. It shows a lack of due diligence. And this information gap creates a mammoth opportunity on which charlatans and Jehovah's Witnesses prey.

While growing up, I fantasized about telling Mama that she needed to challenge Club doctrine. I would quote Proverbs 13:16, "Every prudent man acts out of knowledge, but a fool exposes his folly."

She would disregard that scripture and quote 1 Corinthians 1:19: "For it is written: 'I will destroy the wisdom of the wise; the intelligence of the intelligent I will frustrate.'"

Then I would say, "Anybody can quote the Bible to prove anything, which is why you ought to worry about being so over-confident." But I also knew that I couldn't argue with Mama—a well-programmed true believer. She was trained to believe that only the Club interprets the Bible correctly.

Even when Mama went in the door-to-door work, she would ask potential converts, "Would you like to have a better understanding of the Bible? To know what God wants you to do to earn everlasting life?" The assumption was that she understood the Bible; she had all the answers, when in fact she only knew what the Club told her. This is the blind following the duplicitous. While it doesn't work on everyone, the responses scripted out by the Club's leadership have been purchased, sight unseen, by millions of adult JW converts around the world.

Sincere JWs will look you in the eye and unblinkingly tell you that their group, and only their group, knows and understands the Bible. That God's Holy Spirit entrusts the Club's legal organization, the Watchtower Society, with the sole interpretation of its sixty-six books. It gives them the right to cherry pick what's relevant revelation to people in today's world.

But Jehovah's Witnesses are totally ignorant about what many Bible scholars, Christian seminaries, historians, scientists and archeologists have been reporting about the Bible for the past two hundred years. Here are just a few of the reported discoveries that I would have liked to share with Mama on that first visit back to Nebraska as an ex-JW:

- The Old Testament consists of thirty-nine books written by dozens of authors over six hundred years, or maybe more. Moses did not write the first five books. In fact, it is hard to know if he ever existed.

- The account of Creation in Genesis 1 is very different from the account in Genesis 2. Not only is the wording and writing style different (particularly when read in Hebrew), but the two chapters actually use different names for God, and the content differs greatly.
- We do not have the original writings of the New Testament. What we have are copies of these writings, made years later—in most cases, many years later.
- Not one of these copies is completely accurate since the scribes who produced them inadvertently and/or intentionally changed them in places. Sometimes they didn't mean to—they were simply tired, or inattentive, or on occasion, inept. At other times, though, they meant to make changes, as when they wanted the text to emphasize precisely what they personally believed about the nature of Christ, or about the role of women in the church, or about the wicked character of their Jewish opponents. (In the 1950s, Jehovah's Witnesses rewrote the Bible, calling it The New World Translation, to make it fit their unique beliefs. So it should not come as a surprise that this type of thing happened many, many times in the long history of the Bible.)
- The creation of the Christian canon was not the only invention of the early Church. A whole range of theological perspectives about the nature of God—the formulation of Christian theology—came into existence. Not during the life of Jesus or even through the teachings of his original apostles but later, as the Church grew and transformed into a new religion rather than a sect of Judaism.
- The authors of the New Testament actually have differing views about Jesus and how salvation works.
- We don't know for sure who wrote the four Gospels: Matthew, Mark, Luke, and John. These books were originally written anonymously and not by any of the apostles. All of the original twelve apostles were illiterate, so they could not read or write.
- The New Testament may contain at least seven books that were forged in the names of the apostles by Christian writers who lived decades later.

- The New Testament was written by sixteen or seventeen authors over a period of seventy years. Only eight of the twenty-seven books are written by the people traditionally thought to be the authors. Most of the books are written not by apostles, but by later writers *claiming* to be apostles.

- When Paul wrote his letters (penned before the Gospels) to the churches he founded, he didn't think he was writing the Bible. So, too, with the Gospels. The author of Mark had no idea his book (the first Gospel to be written) would be put into a collection with three other books and called Scripture. He did not think that his book should be interpreted in light of what other Gospel writers would write some thirty years later in different countries and in a different context.

- There is only one book in the New Testament, 1 Timothy — *forged in Paul's name by someone living later* — that states that a woman's place in the church is to be silent and to "exercise no authority over a man." What's amazing is that this policy is clearly at odds with the books that Paul really did write, as well as what he preached and practiced.

- The twenty-seven books of the New Testament were not gathered into one canon and considered scripture, finally and ultimately, until hundreds of years after the books and letters themselves were first produced.

I share this generally accepted information about the Bible because I think it makes better sense if readers acknowledge inconsistencies in the Bible. Staunchly insisting there are absolutely no contradictions within its pages, like Mama and members of the Club do, makes a person vulnerable to misinformation and manipulative religious leaders.

Breaking the News to Mama
Chapter 10

In spite of my lack of knowledge about the history of the Bible in November 1965, I planned to explain my reasons for leaving the Club to Mama. It would also be my first trip back to Nebraska with my wife and son, as an official nonmember of the Club. And I had a good job waiting for me on my return with my self-esteem at an all-time high.

Four months earlier, Mama had stayed with us in our Hamilton home to attend Tim and Esther's wedding. She had no idea of my limited Club activity since leaving Bethel and was unaware that I planned to resign. During that visit, Mama made a mean-spirited remark that Helen still smarted from. It happened shortly after she arrived when the two of them were alone in the kitchen and Helen asked, "Mom, would you mind setting the table for dinner?"

"Listen Helen, I'm not your mother, and I don't want you calling me Mom. Just call me Gail."

Those two sentences cut to the quick. Mama just erased any potential that Helen would be a confidante to her new mother-in-law. There would be no sharing of information or ganging up on me between the two of them, although this wasn't Helen's style anyway. Other than talking with Fred Rusk shortly after we were married, Helen remained tight-lipped about my spin on the Club and my inactivity.

After we arrived at my parents' home, I agreed to go to the

Thursday meeting later that night. Mama wanted to show off her grandson, and I wanted to see several people at the Hall. To start the meeting, the presiding minister asked me to say the prayer. That took me by complete surprise. I hesitated for a second and thought about the negative vibes my refusal would create. I had prayed hundreds of times before, so I closed my eyes and said what may have been the shortest prayer ever delivered in a Kingdom Hall. But, I decided to break the news to Mama after the meeting in her living room.

Three hours later, when it dawned on Mama that I had left the Club and turned in a resignation letter, she looked pale. "Why?" she screamed.

"Because I don't believe it, and I never have."

"Are you telling me that after spending time at Bethel, you couldn't see this is God's organization?"

"Listen Mama, if I believed like you before going to Bethel, my experience there would have been enough to convince me that this is a man-made—a very flawed man-made—organization."

"But surely, Dickie, you have to admit that we are living in the last days. Bible prophecy is being fulfilled every day. Armageddon is very near."

"Mama, I'm sorry, but I don't believe it."

"Well, what do you believe?"

"I'm not certain. I need to work that out."

As we talked, everyone had gone to bed except Mama and me, our long talk clearly an exercise in futility. Mama didn't have a chance of saying something that would change my mind, and yet she thought some kernel of truth would shake me to my senses. Finally I said, "Listen, I have to go to sleep. If you want to talk more, we can tomorrow." I stood up and walked to my bedroom.

Helen was sleeping when I tucked myself in, the conversation with Mama buzzing in my head. When I confronted Mama with the fact that she told me the world would end before I reached twenty, she denied it. When I shared bits of Club history about the adulterous adventures of the Club's first two presidents, she called them lies. When I reminded her about the double standards at Bethel, she rationalized it as the work of imperfect men. Again and again, she rebutted anything I said that she didn't want to believe. Thoroughly brainwashed, nothing I could say would change her mind. But I felt relieved that I had finally stood up to her. While it had no impact on her, I was at peace with myself.

An Inability to Think for Myself Would No Longer Haunt Me

Late Friday evening, Mama still hoped she could change my mind. This time, she tried to put me on her love-your-Mama guilt trip. How could I be so insensitive? Why don't you want to live with me in the new world? If I continued my current ways, that wouldn't happen. Convinced that she would be living on a paradise earth in her lifetime, that she would never experience death, she wanted me to be there, to live forever in paradise with her. If I went to Jehovah in prayer and asked Him to open my heart, Mama knew I would change my mind. Again, I tried to reason with her, but to no avail.

It was a long twelve-hour drive back to Michigan, but a relief to be free of Mama's senseless harangues. While Helen and I didn't agree on religion, Helen respected my right to decide. She never argued doctrine or harassed me with senseless Bible quotes taken out of context, as Mama would do.

As I drove home, my thoughts turned from Mama to my new job. While I was excited about doing work that I had never done before, I had no idea how my employment at this manufacturing company, now in its declining years, would dramatically change my life, and that of my immediate family.

Clipper Belt Lacer Company
Chapter 11

November 8, 1965, marked my first day on the job as an entry-level factory worker at Clipper Belt Lacer Company. It eventually changed both my life and that of the company significantly.

I had no previous factory experience or knowledge of how this or any business worked. My new employer manufactured and sold yesterday's technology. Sales had been steadily declining year after year for the last thirty years, and the average age of its forty-two employees was fifty-seven. The company could no longer attract the kind of employees it needed to reverse its downward trend. There didn't appear to be a bright future for Clipper or my relationship with it.

I spent my first week at Clipper in a dreary factory, most of the machinery driven by vintage 1915 line shafting and leather power-transmission belts. The hieroglyphic history of this elderly company was scarred deeply into its original non-lacquered wooden factory floors. For years, no money had been spent on paint, lighting fixtures, or the rusting, contorted window frames. The broken seals on most of the glass panels made it nearly impossible to see outside. It hardly allowed what little sunshine west Michigan is allotted during the winter months to creep inside. Ugly oil spills encircled every production machine in the factory. A blue haze generated from cheap cigars and cigarettes lingered menacingly in the areas where the smokers worked—and smokers outnumbered nonsmokers by two to one.

After ten days on the job, I had learned how to calculate the tensile strength of incoming wire. I personally rejected over a thousand pounds of brittle wire, helping me appreciate the value of measureable quality-control standards. I learned to operate a proprietary Rube Goldberg machine—a multitasking machine that folded paper, punched holes, glued a reinforcing strip and printed product information all at once. For someone with no mechanical skills, I thought there might be hope for me after all. My supervisor told me that he had never seen anyone learn so much so quickly and that comment definitely fueled my self-esteem.

On the last day of my second week of work, while learning a secret process the company used to increase the life of rawhide connecting pins, an office clerk informed me that the plant superintendent, John VandenBout, wanted to see me right away. Near quitting time, this was not a good sign. Were they going to let me go? I hoped not since I really liked the work and the people there.

When I arrived at John's office, he welcomed me and closed the door. His big smile, along with a newly lit cigar in his hand, signaled that it might not be bad news. He was not alone. The company's cost accountant and inventory control clerk, Harold Osterbaan, sat near John's desk. He, too, wore a big smile. I took the open seat next to the door and John began, "Dick, an opportunity here at Clipper has just opened up. Our treasurer, Ken Thayer, wants to retire and Harold here has agreed to replace him. That means we have a vacancy for Harold's old job. I think you would be a good candidate. What do you think?"

I was stunned at the swiftness of the offer. When I interviewed with John, he had hinted at the possibility. But I thought it might be six to twelve months away. While it would be an adventure, it was exactly what I wanted. So that's what I told John without hesitation. He asked me to report to work on Monday wearing a suit and tie. John also wondered if I knew of someone who might be interested in my old factory job. He said we needed more young blood at Clipper and I told him that I'd give it some thought and report back to him.

When I arrived home, my mind swirled with excitement. I bear-hugged Helen immediately and challenged her to come up with better news than mine. Now as excited as I, she said, "Tell me, tell me! What happened?"

"I just got a big pay raise!" I picked up Keith from his crib, swung him around, and said, "Your daddy is going to work in an office and wear a suit and tie."

After explaining to Helen what I'd be doing in my new job, she barraged me with questions. Once it had sunk in, I told her that I had more good news. Clipper needed to hire a replacement for my old job, someone with good technical skills. I had thought about it on the drive home. My brother Tim could be that guy.

While Tim and I never saw eye-to-eye on religion, I knew that he was an excellent worker, a fast learner. When Tim worked in maintenance at the Bethel Home, his supervisor once asked me if we had a younger brother. He really liked Tim's technical skills and work ethic, saying "We could use more like him at Bethel."

So I called Tim immediately, giving him the job description and pay rate. I told him that it would be a significant step up from his current job at Roamer Yachts. He liked the idea, but he wanted to talk it over with Esther. Thirty minutes later he called and said he wanted to give it a go, that it sounded like a great opportunity. I told him I'd schedule a job interview for him on Monday if I could.

Tim met with John VandenBout Monday afternoon. I don't know what John asked my brother, but it ranked as John's shortest interview in the fifteen years that I worked with him. Tim passed his physical that day and started work a week later. Thus began a pattern of hiring competent young men, members of the Club, which would help shape my career and the success of Clipper in the future.

While I had dissociated myself as a member of the Club, I still met with members in social settings because of Helen. This allowed me to observe young men not allowed to attend college who had the aptitude for higher learning. If I met someone who fit that description, I made it a point to get to know him, to evaluate his potential work ethic. When a person doesn't think he is being interviewed, it's amazing what you can learn from and about him.

During my work years at Clipper, or until 1981, I hired twenty Club members like Tim. More often than not, they were valuable assets to the company.

My first two years in the factory office was like going to college and getting paid for on-the-job classes in cost accounting, machine-shop scheduling, inventory control and human behavior. I learned how to evaluate and motivate employees. I mastered the basics of how to design and manufacture quality mechanical fasteners (wire hooks), lacing machines, cutters, and connecting pins—our company's core products. I collected advice from our long-term employees, salesmen, customers and suppliers. Harold Osterbaan, our new treasurer, shared information about Clipper's financial position and he told me, off the record, how he thought the company should be run.

As rich as that education was, I did not do all of my learning on the job. After my first year, I enrolled in a correspondence school in Chicago, ultimately earning an accounting degree. I attended night school at a local college. I enrolled in a Dun & Bradstreet training course to learn about credit management.

While I enjoyed my work and was paid well, Harold told me it was only a matter of time. Clipper sold buggy whips to a market that wouldn't be around in ten years. He had heard the scoop personally from Clipper's president.

A Rich Man's Family
Chapter 12

In November 1966, I had been a Clipper employee for one year. Helen and I were happy with our lives. And my dissociation from the Club had not harmed our marriage. I still received regular letters from Mama asking me to come back to the Truth. Even today at ninety years of age, she cannot believe how anyone can really be happy if she or he is not a JW.

Eight months after I started my job at Clipper, Helen and I decided that Keith would not be an only child. So baby-making became a high priority at our house. And it didn't take us long to get the job done, thinking the baby would come in August 1967. However, in June Helen's belly was so big that I thought about taking a Japanese language class; she had to be carrying a future Sumo wrestler. After Helen's June checkup, the doctor told her that the baby could come early, to be prepared to go to the hospital at any time.

Helen called her mother with this news. Would she be available to help us? Keith, now two, would need someone to look after him when we were at the hospital. Pleased that we asked, Gertrude said it would be an honor to take care of him. That's what grandmas are for.

When Helen had her next checkup on July 5, 1967, she had already started dilating. The doctor wanted her in the hospital right away. His office called me at work with that news. I told my fellow workers at Clipper about the new development and then I called and talked with Helen's mother.

"Gertrude, this is Dick. There's been a change in plans. Helen's in the hospital. The doctor said the baby will come very soon. Probably in the next twenty-four hours. How early can you get to the house?"

It took a while for Gertrude to respond and I wondered if we had been disconnected. Then, "Oh Dick, I am so sorry but I won't be able to help you. It's such a shame, but the (Club district) assembly is being held in Lansing for the next three days. It's very important that I be there. Hopefully, you can find someone else to take care of Keith."

Speechless at first, but knowing Gertrude, I realized she wasn't joking. Like, "Oh, I'm just kidding, you know I'll be there." Her Club-trained conscience had trumped family, making attending an assembly far more important to her. It's what God would have wanted her to do.

I didn't say a thing and counted to ten. Then without saying another word to Gertrude, I slammed the phone into the receiver and seethed.

Stan Cook, our product design engineer, sat working at the drafting table directly behind me. He could see and feel my agitation and politely asked, "Is something wrong with the baby?"

"No, it's my damn mother-in-law. She's a religious fanatic. Oops, sorry about that, Stan. I shouldn't talk like that."

I wanted to rant to Stan about what had just happened, but knew better. However, it didn't stop me from pondering why Helen's mother could not see how poorly she had behaved. This had to be a no-brainer for anyone with the ability to think. My God, it's family, too. Unfortunately, that's what happens when a person donates their critical thinking skills to the Club, The Watchtower Bible & Tract Society.

An Inability to Think for Myself Would No Longer Haunt Me

I thought about telling Gertrude how much she had disappointed me, but it would have accomplished nothing. Once people get involved in a cult, thinking or seeing themselves as others see them is erased by *the group's delusional definition of how to love God*, clearly defined in black-and-white terminology.

Fortunately, one of our non-JW neighbors helped us out at the last minute. So within twenty-four hours, I went from one of those low points of my life—Gertrude's dagger—to one of the happiest moments in my life—the birth of our second child.

I had heard from Clipper workmates that married couples with a son and a daughter had a rich man's family. So when someone asked if I wanted a boy or girl, I would say: "I'd like to have a rich man's family." Clinging to that mindset, the nurses shooed me out of Helen's Blodgett Hospital birthing room, reporting that the baby wanted out now. If my wish came true, our daughter's name would be Kimberly Joan Kelly.

I waited several hours before the doctor walked into the waiting room. He was followed by a nurse, who carried a newborn baby. I excitedly stood up, my heart beating rapidly. With a big, proud smile on his face, the doctor announced, "Mr. Kelly, you have a new, healthy baby girl."

With tears of joy streaming down my face, I could not have imagined a better gift. While she was still covered with a thin layer of afterbirth, it didn't stop me from planting a big kiss on my daughter's adorably delicate, pinkish-red face—another one of those moments in life that I will never forget.

While forty-four years have passed, I remember well my unrelenting excitement bringing Helen and Kim to our apartment for the first time. I could not wait to introduce our daughter to her big two-year-old brother, a sweet memory. Then to see the surreally contented look on Keith's face when he first caught sight of Kim and how his eyes flashed with approval—it doesn't get more spiritual than that for me.

All went well for our young family until I received a telephone call from Helen's sister Ellie in December 1968. Ellie thought it best to call me, and for me to break the news, the bad news, to Helen. Their father had just died of a massive heart attack.

I sat stunned in my office chair for several minutes. Pop had retired in June at age sixty-five. While bone skinny, he still enjoyed foods high in unsaturated fats and bad cholesterol. He had diabetes and could not break his lifelong addiction to smoking unfiltered cigarettes. It didn't help that Gertrude's unbridled enthusiasm to convert him could turn into virulent guilt-tripping and name-calling exercises. She did this twice in my presence. Both times it triggered a red-faced frenzy in Pop that made me think he could die on the spot.

When I was alone with him, he appeared to be comfortable with me. I never told him that I had dissociated myself from the Club. But somehow, I knew he knew. Earlier in the year, we had an interesting conversation about his pirouetting daughter. He admired her disposition and wished he could be more like her. She did not take negative comments or put-downs as seriously as he did. Helen saw the best in people, preferring to dance joyously through life. Oh, how he wished he could have been more like her.

Breaking the news of Pop's death to Helen would not be easy. I called and asked her to sit down. I had some bad news. Her dad had just died of a heart attack. No reaction, just a long silence. Like the brain taking its time to evaluate the news. Then she began to cry hysterically. I knew that I had made a mistake. I should have talked with her in person. So I left work immediately, arriving at our house in thirty minutes.

Kim was crying because her mother was crying, not yet old enough to understand the finality of death. But that wasn't the case with her three-year-old brother. He wanted to know what had happened. How could he help his mom? What will Grandma do without Grandpa? It was a significant moment in his life. This event and future new truths revealed by the Club, shaped in un-intended ways Keith's and his sister's beliefs about the purpose of life and life after death. It would serve them well when they became adults and parents.

But it would not happen without conflict, the kind of conflict that can and does break most families.

The Problems Begin
Chapter 13

When a religious group is governed and controlled by old men who have never had children and believe fervently that women are second-class citizens, its decisions and policies will be fatally flawed. No one should have to explain this phenomenon to a rational person. But believers trapped in the Club cannot see it. At some point, they aren't able to recall when their cognitive thinking skills, or any semblance thereof, were psychologically removed. They are trained to be comfortable with allowing church leaders to do their thinking, as oppressive as those leaders' decisions may be.

The Ghost of Inadequacy Makes it Difficult to Think for Oneself

One of the Club policies that reflects this disconnect is *infants should go to five one-hour meetings every week with their parents.*

When you have two totally devoted members, perhaps it makes sense. But when you have a nonbeliever willing to stay home and babysit while the believer attends the meeting, one would think this would be a good solution. Fortunately, after Keith was born, Helen agreed with me on this point.

Unfortunately, shortly after Helen's father died, it became an issue. Helen wanted to start taking Keith and Kim to some of the meetings. We finally reached a workable agreement: she would take the kids with her to the Sunday meeting. But a year later, the Club reported that new truths had been revealed to its leadership. It now recommended that children in divided families attend all the meetings with the believing parent. We argued long and hard over this one, before Helen finally decided to compromise.

Just when it appeared we had a workable plan, new issues popped up. What happens if the kids need a blood transfusion? Will they have to refuse to salute the flag when they go to school? What if they don't want to attend meetings or go to assemblies with their mom? Could they celebrate their birthdays or holidays? And the Club's convoluted interpretations of the Bible triggered many last-minute surprises.

One of those surprises occurred during a summer vacation in 1969. We had driven to California with Tim and Esther the year before, meeting with several JW families that Tim and I knew while growing up, never discussing my dissociation from the Club. But I learned on the trip that several of my boyhood JW friends were no longer members, although still married to JWs. That piqued my interest and I made plans to visit Steve Lassos and John Hoyle and their immediate families the following year.

Helen and I drove alone to California this time, leaving Keith and Kim with my parents in Nebraska. Helen knew both Steve and John were no longer JWs and she was okay with that. But the day before our visit with John, she learned from Steve's wife, Pam, that John had just been disfellowshipped. Immediately, she wanted to cancel the visit. It would be a sin to spend time or talk with him. After a heated two-hour debate, we reached a compromise. Helen and I would make the visit because John's wife, Julie, and their three daughters would be there as well. Helen rationalized that she would be visiting with them and not John.

Shortly after that, I voted for the first time. By voting, at least per Club rules and regulations, I had rejected God's Kingdom. Set up in 1914 with Jesus Christ as its king, total allegiance needed to be given *this* government—a theocracy capably managed here on earth by, of course, the Club. Needless to say, voting counts as a significant sin if you're a good Club member. Not being a member, my conscience had not been compromised. I also didn't think it necessary to flaunt the differences in how Helen and I believed, so I didn't tell Helen that I had voted.

Deciding not to tell Helen would have worked except that the polling took place at a local grammar school. The son of the presiding elder at the Hall that Helen attended saw me and told his father. At the next meeting, the elder cornered Helen and had a long talk with her about my sin—an offence for which I could be disfellowshipped. My resignation letter did not free me from Club rules. Baptized at age ten made me a JW. Once a JW, always a JW, according to Club theology.

After Helen confronted me with my crime, I made it clear that I would vote again. I did not stop her from going to meetings and she shouldn't try to stop me from voting. After a volatile conversation, I called the elder and told him what I had told Helen. He could disfellowship me right now, because I would vote again!

Surprisingly, he backed off, confessing that he did not always see eye-to-eye with some of the Club's policies. No one but his son had seen me vote. There needed to be two witnesses to my crime. So per his conscience, I could get off on a technicality. He recommended that I vote in the future when school children weren't present at the polls. His conciliatory demeanor totally diffused my anger, at least for the time being.

When Keith was four, Helen and I came to a long-term agreement which was quite remarkable on her part, given the nature of the Club's intransigent beliefs. Our kids would go to the meetings and assemblies with Helen if they wanted to go. She could study the Bible with them. They wouldn't be forced to *not* salute the flag, although we wouldn't celebrate holidays. She would try to raise the kids as Jehovah's Witnesses but in the end they would have a choice. They would receive blood transfusions if necessary and they couldn't be baptized until they were adults. Keith and Kim would be taught that religious beliefs were personal decisions based on spiritual needs. I didn't love God less, nor were my actions and beliefs controlled by the Devil because I wasn't a Jehovah's Witness. Both kids would go to college.

This worked well for several years. I spent regular one-on-one time with Keith and Kim while they were growing up, encouraging them to think for themselves. We championed the value of science, unbiased history, art, and math in our home. Both Helen and I encouraged them to do well at school. Getting a good education would be critical if they wanted to be qualified for a well-paying job, one they enjoyed as adults. And Helen was the kind of mother every child should have, caring and nurturing. But her very legalistic religion, that gave us problems.

One of my flaws, not keeping my mouth shut at the dinner table in front of the kids, only aggravated the problems. We could be having a nice conversation and without malice, Helen would suddenly change the subject and share something she learned from *The Watchtower.* I suspect the kids could have cared less. But, I'd get this urgent need to set the record straight so everyone knew that misinformation is misinformation. Then I'd go off on a tangent, which embarrassed me much more than Helen. Afterwards, I'd kick myself because it was obvious that Keith and Kim saw my behavior as picking on Mom.

One of the Manifestations of The Ghost of Dependency Haunting Me

I would also show my hostility in other irrational ways, behavior symptomatic of my need to control. Helen was entitled to her opinion, even if it was shaped in many ways by the Club. But my outbursts in front of the kids only made the problem worse.

Some things were never discussed in front of the kids. One of those had to do with sex. The Club is very aggressive with its advice about what married couples can and cannot do in their bedroom. I was really infuriated when Helen told me—no, showed me in *The Watchtower*—why we would no longer have sex when she had her period. It was a newly revealed truth from the Club and she would be breaking God's law if she persisted. Nothing I could say or do would change her mind.

Several months later, Helen learned a new truth at a Club convention. YMCA members were guilty of idolatry and would be disfellowshipped. The YMCA was now considered to be part of Babylon the Great, the great whore referred to in the Book of Revelation and branded as another one of the false religions controlled by the Devil and his demons.

I had been a member of the Grand Rapids YMCA for eight years, a place to swim and exercise. I attended no church services there. But it made no difference. God had chosen the Club as His channel and Helen believed Club mandates. She asked me to quit. I refused. So she tattled to the presiding elder at her Hall, the same elder I had talked with about voting five years before.

He called me right away and let me know that there wouldn't be any wiggle room this time. If I did not resign as a YMCA member, I'd be disfellowshipped. I told him that he should do what his conscience dictated and hung up.

His conscience and subsequent plan amounted to convincing Helen to persuade me to find another place to exercise. This would make it a nonissue. He told her about gyms with better facilities. She should convince me that a change of scenery in my exercise routine would be in our best interest. And it worked, although it marked another intrusion in my life. My resentment continued to build.

In 1974, additional new truths from the Club were revealed to Helen from *The Watchtower*. Again, more things that we could and could not do in our bedroom. It didn't make any difference that I agreed with most of the taboos. I found Helen's continued willingness to allow the Club into our bedroom very offensive, hardening my resentment for her poor judgment.

Keith was nine and Kim seven at the time. So I submerged myself in work. I increased the time I spent playing softball and started jogging five to ten miles a day. I played tennis more. My morality, *at least not yet*, and my work ethic were never in question. I would always love Helen. I just didn't know how I could go on living with one of Jehovah's Witnesses.

My disgust, very open at times, for Helen's Club-trained conscience started to gnaw on her. She began to focus more on my flaws, as unhappy with me as I was with her. Because she allowed the Club's rules, regulations and guilt to influence many of her decisions about our marriage, I began to see her as a burden. Yes, she was a good mother to my kids, but I wanted a soulmate.

To make matters worse, well-meaning Club members attempted to void the long-term agreement between Helen and me. When Keith and Kim were old enough, several of their JW relatives began writing letters to them. They called on the phone. Sometimes they delivered the message in person. They were intent on warning Keith and Kim that the end of this old world was imminent. My two children needed to go to the meetings and read *The Watchtower* if they didn't want to be destroyed at Armageddon.

The Ghost of Misinformation Reporting that Keith & Kim Will Die at
Armageddon Unless...

This was all done behind my back. When I learned about specific incidents, I would accuse Helen of complicity. She had some responsibility to help keep our agreement. Unless we made significant changes, our marriage was headed for a meltdown.

Further Reflections
Chapter 14

As I reflect today on this trying time in my marriage, I could have acted more responsibly. It's not like the storm clouds appeared out of nowhere. They had been forming for years and were not going to disappear on their own. But still, I did not know then about the existence of ghosts—elusive, haunting ghosts—that I had harbored from my sixteen years while growing up as a Jehovah's Witness.

I also did not realize the significant sway that Gertrude began to hold on Helen's life, in particular after Helen's father died. Gertrude strongly believed my dissociation from the Club put her daughter's eternal life in jeopardy. Unable to confront me personally, she used all of her maternal guile to protect Helen.

Gertrude proved to be a formidable opponent. She used every opportunity to remind Helen that they could be in paradise together if Helen towed the mark, adhering to strict Club guidelines. She might even save me by her good conduct. The key: stay resolute. One did not rationalize Club beliefs or question God's organization on earth. Believers must assume they were always right if they wanted to live forever in God's new world.

Like Mama, Gertrude could be very believable if one listened to her with an uncritical ear. She never doubted that her *expectation of things hoped for* would become a reality. She oozed confidence. She wanted—no, needed—to believe that she and her children would never die. She believed it possible if they stayed loyal to God. Which of course meant she and her children had to do what the Club said to do in *The Watchtower* and at her meetings at the Kingdom Hall.

Gertrude also manipulated her adult children with aggressive and subtle doses of guilt. Who doesn't love their mother? She artfully connected herself with Jehovah God. If you pleased God, you pleased Gertrude. What Gertrude liked, God liked.

Gertrude had been a good mother to her five children. But when Helen turned thirteen, Gertrude found the Truth. Converting Helen and her younger sister had been relatively easy. Converting her husband, Hank, proved to be another story.

Gertrude strongly believed that if Hank acquiesced, the other three kids would follow. Unfortunately for her, it never happened. For ten years, she took it personally that Pop couldn't believe. Then he suddenly died, not yet a JW. Gertrude needed to make sure this didn't happen with any of her five children. So she engaged on a serious mission, a mission that would interfere with my marriage to Helen, and I compounded the problem by clinging to a *concept*, a key bit of Club misinformation.

I struggled with my misguided belief that "the truth" could be found. Not the truth as the Club defines it, but some ultimate truth about my life and all living things. Somebody had it, but who and what? I thought if I worked hard enough, it would be possible to find the eternal truth about God, man's destiny, the Bible and life after death. I knew who didn't have the truth, but that didn't help.

The Ghost of Inadequacy or Intellectual Irresponsibility Hard at Work

My misguided belief that some church was the repository of the ultimate truth stymied my progress. The truth is I should have been looking for *good questions to ask about the ultimate nature of man and his insecurities. The Ghost of Misinformation* was alive and well, as I could not yet grasp Lord Tennyson's words of wisdom, "There lives more faith in honest doubt, believe me, than in half the creeds."

The Nasty Ghost of Misinformation

While growing up in the Club, I was constantly bombarded with the claim that it, and only it, has *the truth*. Ex-members, gone for twenty years, will confess, "Oh, I left the Truth years ago." They left because they were no longer believers, and yet those words, the Truth, are ingrained in their psyche. I too, had not figured it out.

I am convinced that *Misinformation*, and its many components, is the most haunting of the ghosts I acquired from my JW experience. And I am not alone. The prodigious amounts of *things that ain't so* that people acquire while in a cult boggles the mind. It skews how they see the world, history, themselves, other people, the arts, science, politics and religion. Being aware of that fact is only half the battle. Shedding oneself of that misinformation is a long, arduous task. Were I to leave the Club today, given that I could read at a high school comprehension level, my recovery plan would be to read the following six books, in this order, and here's why:

1. *Man's Search for Meaning* by Viktor E. Frankl. The author gives a moving account of his life in Nazi death camps and his discovery of logotherapy—a positive approach to the mentally/spiritually disturbed person. His treatment focuses on the freedom to transcend suffering and find a meaning to one's life regardless of circumstances.
2. *The Source* by James A. Michener. A great bit of storytelling based on factual data about early civilization in Israel, debunking JW myths.
3. *The God Delusion* by Richard Dawkins. Okay, he's an atheist, but a person coming out of a group like JWs will appreciate and relate to his hard-hitting, factual observations about the imbecilities of religious fanatics and the dangerous rise of superstition in today's world. (This is a good book to test one's ability to hold two opposed ideas in their

mind and still retain the ability to function, F. Scott Fitzgerald's "test of a first-rate mind.")

4. *Jesus, Interrupted – Revealing the Hidden Contradiction in the Bible* by Bart D. Ehrman. Most Christians are completely in the dark as to what scholars have been saying for 200 years about Bible history, forgeries, and contradictions. Whichever side a person sits on biblical accuracy, this is an eye-opening read.

5. *The Sins of Scripture* by John Shelby Spong. This book exposes the evil done by people who use the Bible like weapons in the name of God. It points out texts that have been used to discriminate, oppress and distort the truth of Christianity, casting doubt on God's love.

6. *Why Evolution is True* by Jerry A. Coyne. I hate the title, but this well-written explanation by a knowledgeable scientist is a fresh, nonthreatening perspective of how old our earth is and how new species evolved from previous ones. And it makes a good case for the fact that God is not a micromanager, as JWs claim.

If people once involved in a cult will read these books, they will be amazed at how refreshing and energizing basic science and unbiased history can be. Not only will they rid themselves of toxic misinformation, but it will also be like getting a good liberal arts college education at a bargain price. For the rest of their lives they will be rewarded with knowing they have acquired "real truths"—liberating, factual information—that had been censored for them. They will have the freedom to decide what *they* want to believe, and can decide based on facts, not superstitious nonsense.

If you're an unabashed Christian and uncomfortable with writers like Dawkins and Ehrman, I have listed books in *Questions & Observations from Readers* that my cousin, Ron Stansell, a retired professor at George Fox University, would recommend reading after leaving a cult.

Now back to my story: If I had then been aware of what I now know about my ghosts, misinformation, and Gertrude's intentions, could I have eliminated an embarrassing chapter in my life? I will never know because that's not how my life played out. I was tested by how well I responded to the impending storm. Not only when it hit, but after it was over.

Bits & Pieces About Helen, Me & My Sanctuary
Chapter 15

Before the eye of the perfect storm implodes in my life, which it will do in the next chapter, I want the reader to know a few disconnected facts about Helen, me, Clipper and my sanctuary. These are bits and pieces—some silly, sad, poignant and *it is what it is*—about people, events and a destination—my sanctuary—that helped shape my state of mind during the coming crisis.

First and foremost, I did not find Helen totally unbearable. We had many good days and for what it's worth, I was slowly developing *a philosophy* about the nature of man, which gave spiritual meaning to my life.

Work life at Clipper was the engine that invigorated me. For thirty years, I never experienced a day that I didn't enjoy. From 1965, when I started, until I sold my shares in the company in 1995, work fueled my self-esteem, giving significant meaning to my life.

Late in 1968, the president of the company retired and my boss, John VandenBout, was appointed the new president. He quickly made several big improvements, championed several of my suggestions, and the company began to grow. In 1969, I became the company's secretary and treasurer and my brother Tim took over my old job in the factory office.

John VandenBout made a strong statement early in his presidency when he convened a special meeting of Clipper's seven outside salesmen. A company-wide sales meeting had not been held in over forty years. John asked me and other key employees to join the group. We discussed problems and opportunities for three days. Many of the salesmen's suggestions on how to attract new business were easy to implement. And within a year, we had doubled our annual sales.

In May 1971, my brother Tim called and asked if he could stop at our house and talk. By the sound of his voice, I had an ominous premonition that what he had to say wouldn't be good. Arriving with a somber look on his face, he asked if we could talk alone on the patio. He told me he planned to quit his job at Clipper. Not because he didn't like his work. His passion had always been full-time ministry—as a special pioneer for the Club. Driven by his belief of a looming Armageddon, he felt God's calling to warn people of the coming holocaust. As special pioneers, Tim and his wife, Esther, would each spend 150 hours a month, canvassing door-to-door for converts. Their assignment from Club headquarters had arrived in the mail that day. In three weeks, they would begin a ministerial experience that would make Tim responsible for a rural congregation in northern Michigan with special needs. They had already put a down payment on a used trailer and found a place to park it. The two of them planned to do janitorial work to supplement the little monthly stipend they would receive from the Club.

What a shock. The planning for this had been in the works for a long time. It's what Tim and Esther wanted, and I couldn't do a thing about it. Finding someone with a comparable work ethic would not be easy. But before Tim left, I had pinpointed a potential replacement—a young man who went to Helen's Kingdom Hall. He had worked a year at Clipper doing menial jobs in the factory, quitting six months before. I called him minutes after Tim left the house. Within twenty-four hours, John Henry Meulenberg called to say that he would accept Tim's old job. Tim spent his last two weeks at Clipper training John.

To Tim's credit, while he lived in west Michigan, he never

discussed religion with me. In stark contrast to Mama, he could accept me without a constant barrage of Club dogma. If I was going to die at Armageddon and that bothered him, he made no effort to let me know one way or the other.

Tim and Esther were assigned to Gaylord, Michigan—a city of 3,000 people, 200 miles north of Grand Rapids. Helen and I went to visit them a year later. While having dinner in their small trailer, Tim told us about things, one in particular, that he didn't like in his new assignment.

"I can't tell you how many times I get calls from sisters at the Hall telling me that their husbands insist on having oral sex. Then I have to talk with the guys, to show them in the Bible why God doesn't approve of it."

I remained silent and carefully listened. Yet, it galled me that the Club deemed it so important that its representatives had to spend time on such matters. Why would Tim consent to tell someone that God didn't approve of blow jobs? Ironically, he answered that question when he said, "I don't like doing it, but it's necessary work if we are to keep the congregation clean and God's spirit flowing smoothly."

By this time, John Meulenberg had shown his mettle by being the catalyst on several product innovations well beyond Tim's reach. John's technical design skills and innate intellectual curiosity made the difference. Even without a college education, he helped develop many new products over the next few years.

Our Customer Service Manager, Craig Blackburn, also attended a local Kingdom Hall. John, Craig and I worked well together. They gave no indication that my being an ex-JW bothered them. In fact, during our hour-and-a-half lunch break at Clipper, we often ate, talked and played cards together. Sometimes during our free time, we went bowling or played billiards. During the summer months, we swam at a nearby lake.

The one problem we had related to our spouses. In social settings, most JW wives are clannish, treating non-JWs like they were unclean. Helen was the exception. And that was good as Clipper's president, John VandenBout, encouraged social interaction with our wives during sales meetings and at directors' meetings. John's wife, Cora, and Helen became good friends from the moment they met. But then everyone liked Helen. In that kind of a social environment, Helen never talked religion. She oozed happiness, spontaneity and joy, her dad's ballerina.

After being at Clipper a year, I enrolled in a Dale Carnegie class, a special type of training that helped me understand how important *attitude* is to a person's potential success in life. *It's your attitude, not your aptitude that determines your altitude* was a slogan that I could embrace. Carnegie's philosophy of positive thinking made perfect sense, my new religion. I read all kinds of books on the subject, including Carnegie's *Lincoln the Unknown*. Abraham Lincoln became my superhero. I read Sandburg's books on Lincoln's life and I learned to speed read.

During a three-year period, I read five books a week, the ultimate escape. But it created a void. I wanted to talk with someone about the things that I was learning. Unfortunately, Helen had no interest in reading these kinds of books. That shouldn't have been a problem. However, I foolishly added this difference to my list of resentments—things I did not like about Helen. I would soon pay dearly for that judgment error.

After we bought our first home in 1969, I had a compelling need to learn more about my biological father, Dean Lowe Geddes. I had never met him. Mama first told me about him when I was sixteen, a week after his pickup truck careened off an icy road, hit a tree in Pocatello, Idaho, killing him. But I knew nothing more about him or his family. Not sure what I'd find, I began to research this man, a man that Mama lived with for three months before the announcement of my conception ended their relationship.

Dean, one of fourteen children, had served honorably during WWII. Married with a baby in Pocatello, he met Mama in Salt Lake City in December 1942—a confirmed bachelor, he said. His parents were now dead, but twelve of his siblings still alive. They were raised in Banida, Idaho, on the other side of the mountain from where Mama grew up in Robin, Idaho.

It took me more than five years to come up with this information. But I wanted to take it a step further. So I asked my cousin, Mark Evans, to make some calls, check things out, to see if any of

Dean's siblings were interested in meeting with me. My Grandma Evans thought it could come to no good. So without telling her what we were doing, Mark discreetly made contact with two of Dean's sisters in 1972. However, when I received a phone call early on a Saturday afternoon, at our home on Royal Oak, it caught me totally by surprise.

I picked up the phone on the second ring and said hello. "Can I talk with Richard Kelly?" I told the woman that she was speaking to him. Then in a clear, strong voice, she said, "Richard, this is your aunt Huitau Geddes Miles, Dean's sister." I paused to take in this awkward but exciting moment. Hearing her voice was surreal, as if I was talking to my biological father by proxy. It was my first link to a family that I had wanted to know about since I was four years old, but Mama had always been tight-lipped about it. Huitau was related to me; we shared the same bloodline. I felt whole, alive and very connected.

"Wow! You found me."

"Richard, we want to meet you. When can you come see us?"

"Oh my, I can tell we're related! You don't have any patience either. Now who are we and us?"

She laughed a hearty Geddes laugh before saying, "Well, Sarah is with me right now. That's Hugh's wife. Then there's Paul, Barta, Scott's wife Lois, June, Grace, Jennie Bon, Lucille, Irel, Garth and Ora. Oh, did anyone tell you that you look just like your dad?"

Talking with Huitau came easy. It seemed so natural and right. A strong, engaging woman, she said she loved me, telling me that over and over again. We talked for thirty minutes. Finally she said that she would get back to me with dates for a family reunion, for the Geddes clan to meet the newest Geddes family member.

Telling this part of my story cannot be told without Helen. While we definitely had significant issues related to religion, there were times in our marriage when I cannot imagine anyone more supportive and understanding. Helen happened to be in the dining room when I picked up the phone. Her intuitive senses tuned in early to this very special moment in my life. She intimately shared the birthing moment when I officially became a part of the extended Geddes family.

After I put the phone down, I excitedly talked with Helen about the experience—an animated conversation with Helen just as excited about my phone conversation with Huitau. Finally, I could exorcise a lifetime of frustration, of not having faces and names of my paternal biological family. Contemplating a meeting with Dean's siblings in person exhilarated me. I hugged Helen again and again, intense hugs. A day, a time in my life, like the birth of my children, which I will never forget.

Our meeting with my biological father's siblings occurred several months later at Uncle Garth's home in Salt Lake City. Seven of my aunts and uncles, along with their spouses, attended the reunion. It's hard to put into words the heartfelt joy, the happy tears that we shed, and poignant stories shared that night. But one fact was not lost on me from that night; I shared this very emotional experience with Helen, even if she was a JW.

During the next five years, we attempted to make up for lost time. I met a half-brother, Cody Geddes. I fell madly in love with my Uncle Irel and his wife Brigitte. And I thoroughly enjoyed the company of every one of Dean's siblings. They met and connected with Keith and Kim. I also introduced Huitau, Grace and Irel to Mama and my step-dad. During our visits with new Geddes family members, I became aware of something special. It's not all nurture that shapes a person. Our interests and personality traits are also shaped deeply by the DNA from our parents and their parents.

While my biological father made many poor decisions in his life, he came from good stock. He may have been scarred, messed up by the impact of combat on the front lines in WWII and a bad first marriage. In the end, we are all responsible for our choices, choices that we have to live with, and choices that other family members should not be held accountable for.

Shortly after our first reunion, I decided to get a copy of my birth certificate. Mama had told me growing up that she had lost it and that getting a copy would be an exercise in futility. Two weeks after mailing my request for a copy, I received it. To my surprise, I was not Richard Evans Kelly. My birth certificate stated my name as *Richard Evans*. However, my social security card reported my name as Richard Evans Kelly, Mama's handiwork. She had done some fibbing and used her preference for my surname. My problem now, I had used Mama's preferred name on my marriage certificate. At age thirty-three, I consulted with an attorney. He told me that I needed to legally change my name to Richard Evans Kelly, which I did. What irony that Helen, Keith and Kim were legally Kellys many years before me.

Mama Willingly Shared Misinformation when it Benefitted Her

Confronting Mama about my legal name brought an interesting revelation. Mama was dating Richard Paul Kelly when I was born and she decided my first name would be Richard. She being an Evans, my legal name, of course was Richard Evans. After Mama married her big Richard, he said that he wanted to legally adopt me. But when they moved to Los Angeles, all their friends assumed me to be his child. So my parents decided to wait. They could use the money on more pressing needs. After they joined the Club, it became a moot point. So convinced were they that Armageddon would come before I reached twenty, they decided that it wasn't necessary for Papa to legally adopt me or change my birth name.

A special destination that significantly impacted my life and that of my family is a sanctuary called The Rocky Mountain National Park near Estes Park, Colorado. In 1966, Helen and I discovered this special place and it was love at first sight. It became my spiritual palace, a vast oasis of mountains, lakes and trails—one of Nature's great wonders. I found it a safe haven, a place to cleanse my mind and body each year. My Mecca. This serene site renewed and empowered me and I shamelessly evangelized about the experience. I proselytized the power of this holy spot to anyone who would listen and I converted many of my friends and family. No one walked away from this mammoth temple without experiencing the real meaning of *awe*.

For thirty successive years after we discovered the Estes Park area, we spent at least one week in the vast expanse of what surely must be one of God's finest sanctuaries. To even think that He spent time in Solomon's man-made temple at Jerusalem is ludicrous to me. But that's what the Club teaches. If you walked a full day on any one of the many spectacular trails in Rocky Mountain National Park, you'd have to be brainwashed or brain dead to believe that God prefers man-made buildings over nature's cathedrals.

My son, Keith, and I climbed to the top of Longs Peak, 14,255 feet, when he was nine years old. Tell me something more real and spiritual than that. You don't think of your problems when you enter into that zone on a long hike in the Rocky Mountains. It's the best church I have ever been to. And no one passes collection plates.

Back in Grand Rapids in the early 1970s, I decided to get involved in politics. My grandparents were lifelong Democrats. To them, a better politician than Franklin Delano Roosevelt did not exist. They considered FDR a saint. So when I decided to become a Jerry Ford Republican, I didn't tell them. I thought of myself as a fiscal conservative and social libertarian, and Ford's politics fit that combination. I wanted to help change the world, to make it better for future generations.

I suspect that some of my motivation to get involved in politics stemmed from defiance against Mama's and the Club's position on politics. (Tell me not to do something and oftentimes that's my motivation to do it.) To the Club, this world is living on borrowed time. It's going out of business. So their position is that a person's time is best spent, not on doing something to make this a better place to live, but to ensure that they will live forever in a world yet to be. I wasn't willing to sacrifice the gift of life that I'd been given, hoping to win God's lottery in a future new world.

I wondered how my getting involved in politics would impact my relationship with Helen. She was dead set against it, as if I would be working with the ultimate enemy—the Devil and his demons. She didn't share my ambitions and had no desire to improve the local and worldwide community for our children or future generations.

Oh, how I hated Helen's religion and her complicity. We were traveling in two different directions. Yes, there were some good moments, but they were getting fewer and fewer, and our marriage was headed for a significant confrontation.

Charlotte
Chapter 16

It appeared that 1977 would be a very good year. Helen and I built a new home. Kim and Keith were doing well in school. I had completed the Grand Rapids 25K Run for a third year, jogged at least five miles a day and was in the best shape of my life. And two uneventful years had come and gone without Armageddon.

The Club's Vice President, Fred Franz, a guy I considered delusional when I worked at Bethel in the early 1960s, had predicted that Armageddon would befall the world in October of 1975. His prediction was published in *The Awake* magazine in 1974. Franz had hinted at those expectations as early as 1969. He shared his convictions at Club assemblies and his doom-and-gloom prophecy became the big buzz by all Club members. Millions of JWs around the world were preparing for the world to be destroyed. So in the mid 1970s, several members called, begging me to come back. Why? So I wouldn't die at Armageddon, as if it'd be okay with God to make a deathbed conversion.

The alarming thing about the 1975 prediction occurred after it didn't happen. JWs, including Helen, denied it. When I showed it to her in print or reminded her of the people who had talked with me about the date, she said it was a big misunderstanding, that it merely revealed a human flaw to want something to happen so badly that Club members—not their leaders—jumped to a conclusion. In Helen's words, "It was *not* bad prophecy by God's organization, the Club."

Continually Being Told You Will Die at Armageddon Unless…

I'd get so frustrated trying to help her see how Club members were manipulated. At the time, I didn't know anything about the power of brainwashing, especially that done by cults. So at times, confusing Helen's convictions with stupidity, I tended to conceal my embarrassment that she believed Club dogma.

Work at Clipper provided a significant escape from my frustration. It was my second year as vice president of the company and business was booming. Clipper had budgeted for a fifty percent increase in sales, due in large part to a fastening system designed for the hay baling market, a product that would revolutionize cattle feeding. We created value for our customers at an affordable price or we went out of business. I liked that kind of straightforward challenge.

One of the biggest challenges to a rapidly growing company is finding capable, passionate employees with the work ethic to sustain momentum. Often people interviewed well, but performed badly. So we developed a strategy of hiring temporary employees. It didn't take long to see if the temps were the kind of employees we wanted for the long term. By this time, we had already hired two people in key positions using this system.

Charlotte, hired early in the year by the inside sales manager, was a highly energetic and very analytical twenty-six year old. After three days on the job, she made several good suggestions on how to improve order-taking. After a week, she could do twice the work of the person she replaced. That caught my attention, so I scheduled a thirty-minute interview and quickly learned that she was overqualified. She had decided to do temp work because she and her husband were new to Grand Rapids for his job as a college professor. Bored, she also planned to take college classes when the new semester started.

I told her that we were pleased with her work and if circumstances changed, she should let us know. I wanted to expand our international business and we needed someone who understood marketing. While she would have to take special classes, I thought she had the aptitude for that kind of work. We would pay for her schooling if she could commit to staying with the company for five years. While flattered, she said that her husband, like many good college professors, was always on the move and she couldn't commit to stay in Grand Rapids for more than two years.

Helen, Keith, Kim and I had a great vacation that summer in Estes Park. Keith and I hiked seventeen miles from Bear Lake, Flattop Mountain, and down the western side of the continental divide—a new spiritual adventure for us. Helen and Kim picked us up near the western entrance of Rocky Mountain National Park. We had good family time together, although we encountered a new road bump. Normally our trips to this mountain sanctuary were a sabbatical from the Club for Helen, but this year she decided to attend service at the small Kingdom Hall on Sunday. I didn't try to stop her, but I wasn't happy. This was not a trend that I wanted to see. Up to now, Club nonsense had been off limits for her in Estes Park.

While hiking near Hallet's Peak, I ran into a longtime friend from Columbus, Nebraska—Emil Marx. Emil had been a neighbor when I went to high school. High on a mountain at 12,000 feet, I learned that he was temporarily out of work as a German teacher in the Denver school system. I asked if he would be willing to come to Grand Rapids for a few months, learn a bit about Clipper's business, and then do a two-week sales trip for the company. I had also targeted two international companies as potential joint venture companies that he could visit. He liked the idea and we made plans for him to come to Grand Rapids in two weeks.

Shortly after returning from vacation, our family moved into our new home. Earlier that year, Helen saw a builder pouring the foundation for a house on Llewellyn Court. We liked the area and wanted a bigger place. It turned out the foundation was for a spec house, and the builder was looking for a buyer; we made an offer and the builder accepted. The home, twice the size of our Royal Oak house, sat on property fenced in by a long dense line of one-hundred-year-old maple and oak trees. Maybe this change of scenery would improve our marriage.

In September, I received a call from Charlotte. She wanted to know about the March job offer. Had we filled it, could she apply? I said that I'd have to check with the sales manager, Craig Blackburn, and get back to her. We talked and decided to hire her. We could use her skills in the Customer Service Department right away. Maybe with some schooling and experience, she might be the person we needed to head our marketing department. We were good at sales, but lacked someone on staff with the analytical skills to set a company-wide strategy that identified, satisfied and kept the kind of customers we wanted. I called Charlotte back the next day and said she could start on Monday; she would report directly to Craig. I'd watch her progress over the next thirty days and come up with a one-year plan to see if she had what it takes.

Charlotte stood 5 feet 4 inches tall and was not a particularly attractive woman, mostly because she did as little as she could to surface her outer beauty. She did not wear makeup, had stocking-cap hair, and dressed dowdily as a personal statement. But inside those secondhand clothes and frumpy frame lived a ball of fire. Her eyes told the real story. They were electric, like sparkling jewels, beaming with a raw, unbridled passion for life. We had discovered a gem waiting to be polished. This young woman had the intellectual and analytical skills that could help the company grow its business. But I wasn't sure how she would make decisions under pressure, and she had a definite chip on her shoulder—a tendency to rant if any guy called her "girl."

After she had worked at Clipper for two weeks, I asked her to stay late. I wanted to get to know her better. What were her aspirations? What did she know about marketing? How good were her research skills? Did she like working behind the scenes, digging up valuable information? How big were her ego needs? Why hadn't she landed a high-level job before? What did she want out of her work and personal life? Could she bite her tongue when she encountered a male chauvinist pig?

Our first interview opened my eyes wide. While undeniably pissed off at the sexist world she lived in, Charlotte had loads of talent. I knew an hour into the conversation that with a little self-discipline, she could be Clipper's first Marketing Manager. We had people on our staff who could sell, but we lacked the talent needed to expand our business internationally, someone who could identify new, growing markets for the products our company manufactured.

When I looked at the clock in my office, almost 7:30 PM, we had been talking for two and a half hours. Shocked at how quickly the time had passed, I stopped and called Helen, telling her that I'd be home late, thinking I would continue to interview Charlotte. But that interruption dramatically changed the dynamics. Charlotte now wanted to interview me. I agreed and suggested we eat and talk at a nearby restaurant. She didn't like the idea. We should have a pizza delivered to Clipper and eat at the large table in the accounting room outside my office.

While Charlotte asked several good questions about Clipper's long-term plans, she wanted to get to know me better. If she invested her future in this company, she wanted to know more about the man who would be leading it. Was I sexist? Was I intimidated by smart women? How did I treat women? Was I intellectually curious? What did I think about religion? What books had I read? What was my wife like? How was I raising my children? What did I think about the women's movement? She also wanted to know why we had so many Jehovah's Witnesses working for the company. Was I a closet JW?

I had never been asked questions like this. Frankly, it felt exhilarating to share my insights on these topics. On some points, I had to dig hard for answers. But what really struck me was that someone was really interested in what I believed. Swept up in this new and refreshing way of relating, I totally lost track of time. When I saw it getting close to midnight, I said that we had to stop. We could continue the conversation during the next few days. She thanked me for my honesty and suggested that she may have finally found a work home, a place where she belonged.

As I drove home, my mind raced with excitement. I believed that Charlotte could be Clipper's first Marketing Manager, although she needed time to get to know the business and our customers. On a personal note, I felt a cathartic sensation, having unloaded a lot of history that I had kept hidden. I felt good about me. I wondered if Helen could one day ask questions like this, to embrace the kind of person I had become and the kind of person I ultimately wanted to be when I grew up intellectually.

Over the next month, Charlotte totally engaged herself in work and learned what made Clipper unique. She joined John, Craig and me at lunch and the chemistry worked. Her off-the-charts skill at questioning was apparent to all of us, a skill she would need to lead the company in marketing. But her zero tolerance for male chauvinism was a red flag that needed to be addressed.

I told her that we needed to talk. She asked to meet after work. I called Helen and said I wouldn't be home for supper. Charlotte and I ordered a pizza and we ate and talked at the accounting table. I expressed my concerns about her lack of anger management. She said she would try to do better in the future, but now was not a good time. She had just gone through an ugly divorce. A divorce she didn't want. She needed time to get balanced. Then she asked if I wanted to play Scrabble. She had a game with her. It seemed harmless and I love the game. While we played, I saw a softer, more sensual side of her. One-on-one, she could be a real lady, and an evening ensued that I could not have imagined, at least not with Charlotte. Suddenly, this frumpy lady turned into an attractive woman. No doubt a response to my vibes, she started flirting with me and I didn't stop her. For the first time, I sensed a special chemistry between us. To make a long story short, events occurred that evening which triggered our sordid journey.

Two months later, I had no doubts that Charlotte and I could have a long-term relationship. I told her that I planned to move out of my house and rent an apartment. This would give us more time together. Then I told Helen I wanted out of the marriage. I'd been unfaithful during the last few months and needed time alone to figure things out. Our marriage didn't appear worth saving with her allegiance to a cult-like religion. Infatuated and not thinking clearly, I told Helen that I would move out of the house immediately. In retrospect, I take full responsibility for not doing what I would figure out four months later.

I also said that she should tell the presiding minister at her Hall that I had broken my marriage vows. He could meet me at Clipper the following weekend and officially disfellowship me. Unlike many JWs, I wanted that badge of distinction. I wanted people to know that I was no longer a JW. The Club could no longer threaten me by saying that if I didn't follow their rules, I would be excommunicated.

Fortuitous for me, in November 1977 and for almost the next four years, the Club relaxed its rules on disfellowshipping. Except for apostasy, a person would not be shunned. This made it much easier for us to reconcile our marriage. It wouldn't be until September 1981 when a new policy would be enacted—a revelation from God—when shunning became a Christian response to anyone disfellowshipped or who voluntarily left the Club.

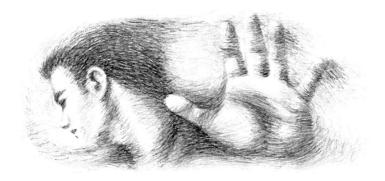

While not always alone when I lived in my apartment, the time away from home gave me an opportunity to reevaluate my marriage. My *aha moment* came while driving with Charlotte. Our destination: Estes Park, Colorado.

Helen had decided to spend the time between Christmas and New Years Day with my brother and her sister, devout JWs in Columbus, Nebraska. Since I couldn't spend time with the kids, I decided to drive to Estes Park and show Charlotte the epicenter of my spiritual world. Risking the potential for some nasty winter driving conditions, we embarked on a 2,300-hundred-mile journey, there and back.

Two days into the trip, I realized that I had made a serious mistake. Not that Charlotte was a bad person or we didn't get along, but that I'd tried to get out of my marriage by entering another. This was not the kind of person I wanted to be. If Helen would take me back, I knew I could reframe my relationship with her. I also knew that I would have to tell Charlotte of my decision; that I planned to end our relationship. It would not be easy. I felt awful, as I had now unnecessarily hurt two good people.

While I would never become a JW to save our marriage, I thought I could address my concerns about Helen's religion in a way that she could decide if our marriage was worth saving. I kicked myself for not figuring it out before deciding to have an affair. But quickly admitting a mistake, at least when I could see it, has served me well over the years.

One of my major concerns, and it really bothered me, was my infidelity. I'm not the kind of person that looks for one-night stands or multiple relationships. Not because it's mandated in some church rules of conduct. I would not want my marriage partner cheating on me. Why would I expect anything less of myself if I wanted a meaningful relationship?

Helen and I began meeting and talking in January 1978 and came to an agreement on what we thought would make our marriage work. I did not ask her to leave the Club or repudiate her religious beliefs. But by the same token, she could not be insensitive to what I believed or didn't believe about God and the hereafter. I made it clear that *we* would decide what went on in our bedroom and not *The Watchtower* or the elders at her Hall. I would never be a JW, so she would have to travel that journey by herself.

Months before, a few days after I had moved out, Helen decided she should start looking for a job. Within two weeks, she found work with the State of Michigan's Motor Vehicle Division. A win-win-win for the State of Michigan, Helen, and me. After a month on the job, she began to take a more tolerant view of non-JWs.

As a JW, she had been taught that anyone not associated

with the Club should be thought of as a *worldly person*. You don't associate with them since they're controlled by the Devil. All Club members must buy into that separation if they're going to be accepted by the Club hierarchy at the Kingdom Hall. And yes, Helen, except for non-JW Clipper employees, had bought into that position. That is, until she started working for the State of Michigan.

The Ghost of Misinformation

Helen is nonjudgmental by nature. She is more than capable of deciding with whom she should and should not associate. Working closely with non-JWs helped her realize that maybe JW hierarchy had caused paranoia, and not God, to enact this harsh policy. Maybe the JWs who were prone to get into trouble, those who needed heavy-duty structure, would find this rule of theocratic law beneficial. Helen decided on her own that not every edict from the Club applied to her. Although it was a small step, I believed she was moving in the right direction.

The Second Time Around
Chapter 17

Making it work the second time around is not an easy emotional transition after one has been unfaithful in a long-term relationship. There's the guilt and the complications, at least in my case, of infidelity with a workmate. Charlotte continued her employment at Clipper after our breakup, although her heart was no longer in her work. Both of us had also come to the conclusion several months before that she did not have the temperament to be the company's marketing manager. While Charlotte's day-to-day presence created additional baggage for me and was a significant challenge for her, I focused on getting my marriage back on track. I wanted it to be a positive experience for Helen, me, and our kids.

Unbeknownst to me, Helen's mom was very upset when she learned that Helen planned to take me back. Gertrude said that if I had cheated on her once, I would do it again. That's what happens when someone leaves the protection of the Club. I had not only abandoned Helen, I had abandoned Jehovah God, which made it worse. When Helen didn't take her advice, Gertrude recommended that Helen at least say the dinner prayer out loud and in front of me and the kids. It would show her loyalty to God and be a good example to Keith, Kim and me.

So at our first dinner meal as a family, Helen abruptly informed us that she would lead the family in prayer at every meal. This news came as a shock. We hadn't agreed to such a plan when we decided to get back together. While she was adamant, even emotional, about the edict, I oddly didn't overreact. I knew immediately that it was our first test. So I said as gently as possible, but with some authority, "Helen, if you want to pray, you'll have to do it silently." The kids looked at me and we waited. It took awhile before Helen responded. "You're right, Dick. I have no right to impose my beliefs upon you." She bowed her head and we waited while she silently prayed. We had passed our first test. Interestingly, Helen never said a silent family-meal prayer again, even though she remained a JW for the next eight years.

Helen continued to work part-time for the State of Michigan and it helped to promote common ground, to make our marriage work. We often attended dinners and get-togethers with her fellow employees, good for both of us. I was Helen's husband, and I liked that. She became good friends with Catholics and Protestants. While not averse to telling workmates her religious denomination, she never tried to preach or convert them. Helen decided that all worldly people weren't bad, as the Club purports. She had eradicated one small appendage of the Misinformation Ghost and gave me a glimpse into the potential alteration of her religious beliefs.

I had been living in my apartment and separated from Helen for a month when I received a letter from Mama. Not happy that I had left Helen, Mama told me that unless I saw the error of my ways and went back home, she would disown me. Ironically, almost four years later the Club told Mama to do just that, even though by then I had clearly demonstrated that I loved my wife and would be faithful to her for the rest of my life.

However, in 1978 when Mama learned that had I reconnected with Helen, she turned out to be one my biggest supporters. I could not have pleased her more. Not alone, several JW employees at Clipper offered support of my decision. My brother and his wife called to congratulate me, as did a few members at the Hall Helen attended. I made a big mistake, but I had seen the error in my ways. I wasn't a womanizer.

Helen, Keith, Kim and I were invited to all the JW picnics after the reconciliation, more so after than before I was disfellowshipped in 1977. We spent quality time with my parents and siblings in Nebraska and Michigan, part of the Club's new policy to kill with kindness. I knew they wanted Keith back. He had decided not to be a JW two years before. While Kim went to the meetings with Helen, she could be lost as well if they stopped associating with us.

I was appointed as the president of Clipper in 1978. My friend Emil Marx's visit to Germany opened the doors for a joint venture with MATO GmbH, a German manufacturer of heavy-duty mechanical fasteners. Early in my presidency, I signed an agreement to sell and service MATO's products to the underground coal mining markets in North America. We started building an additional 30,000 square foot manufacturing facility to support Clipper's rapidly expanding business in the agriculture and package-handling markets. Helen helped wine, dine and host international partners and key customers. Her happy, what-you-see-is-what-you-get attitude made her a valuable asset to Clipper's growing business.

In 1979, President Jimmy Carter asked me to come to the White House. He wanted to put together a nonpartisan group of speakers to rally public support for the SALT II treaty that he hoped to sign with the Soviet Union. Michigan Republicans nominated me and the Democrats picked Coleman Young, the mayor of Detroit. Twelve nominees from six northeast states and the press were invited to the special meeting. While I spent two interesting days at the White House debriefing with Carter and

Zbigniew Brzezinski, the project came to an abrupt halt a week later, when Soviet leader Leonid Brezhnev decided to sign the agreement. I bring this up because Helen supported my involvement. Not something she would have done before our separation, but she knew how important it was to me. She no longer treated my interest in politics as cavorting with the devil.

We were making our marriage work. While Helen and I saw the next world, life after death, very differently, it did no harm to our relationship. While JWs were resolute in their unique spin on religion, it appeared that the failed prediction of Armageddon had taught the Club a valuable lesson. The Club had changed its focus, now on love and forgiveness, a message that Jesus preached, and I could live with that.

But little did Helen and I know that the Club's focus would soon change in a very dramatic and disturbing way. Behind-the-scene maneuvers at the Club's world headquarters would threaten thousands of marriages and families all over the world, including ours, and break up many of them.

Events at the Club's Headquarters
Chapter 19

Much can be said about the schism that began and boiled over at the Club's worldwide headquarters in Brooklyn, New York from 1976 to 1980. It was a consequence of Fred Franz's prediction of Armageddon in1975. While the Club's leadership publicly denied their role in such a flagrant prophetic blunder, a core group of officials at Bethel knew better. How it all played out needs some explanation

Then-president Nathan H. Knorr had been in bad health for months, diagnosed with brain cancer in 1975. He could no longer function in the semi-benevolent dictator role that defined most of his 33-year presidency. Knorr's genius had been to use his own organizational skills and to defer to Fred Franz for divine inspiration. Fred served as the Club's vice-president, resident prophet and self-appointed *It-don't-get-better-than-me* biblical scholar. However, when I worked at Bethel in the early 1960s, only a fool didn't notice that Franz's mental state lacked a motor, crankshaft and both turn signals. President Knorr was not a fool.

So why didn't Knorr replace Freddy Franz? I have a theory. When Knorr and Franz reached their pinnacle of unchecked power, they *really did believe that God talked to them*. Fred in particular. Knorr may have reasoned that God prefers to reveal new truths to odd-looking men with poor social skills. Knorr himself lacked social graces. Since Franz could speak with authority, as if he and

God were buddies, Knorr may have figured Fred's strangeness gave him a God-like aura to the rank-and-file JW.

But remember, Knorr was not a fool. In the mid-1960s, he set up an organizational filter made up of several key men who had the freedom to question Fred's more bizarre predictions and interpretations. One can only speculate why Fred's *Armageddon in 1975* sifted through the filter. But Knorr's organizational strainer had functioned long and well before this slip-up. This group of key men consisted of Gilead instructors, who were not afraid to challenge Fred's megalomaniacal spins, and Fred's nephew, Ray Franz. While Ray had no formal education, he may have been the Club's top Bible scholar during his tenure at Bethel and Fred respected his judgment.

Ray was a unique guy because he had no interest in power, not a threat to those who jockeyed for position in the Club's hierarchy during Knorr's declining years. Ray's passion was love and kindness, not harsh legalistic dictums, believing honey, not vinegar, would attract more followers. Ray wanted the Club to restructure itself to emulate the kind of love he believed Jesus had for his followers.

When Knorr's health began to decline in the mid-1970s, the Club's leadership restructured the organization, well aware of Fred Franz's mental state. Instead of a strong president, management of the Club would be turned over to a Governing Body (GB) with Knorr and Fred as members. Like most skewed Club dogma, this change had been framed so that it appeared to be Bible-based, to make it seem like Jehovah God and not man had come up with this new arrangement. When the idea of a GB was first proposed, both Knorr and Fred protested. It meant the GB, and not the president, would have complete control of the Club's doctrines and policies. But they were powerless to stop it, although Knorr insisted that more hardcore members like him be appointed to the group. So, "Seven of Knorr's *yes men* were called in from outside assignments, asked to live at Bethel and serve on the new GB." (You can read more about Knorr and Bethel life from Randy Watters, a reliable insider's point of view, at www.freeminds.org.)

On January 1, 1976, the GB officially assumed responsibility for managing the Club, a monarchical ruler no longer in charge.

Seventeen old men, including Ray Franz, now controlled the Club's policies. According to *The Watchtower's* spin from that point on, God gave divine revelation to all members on the GB and not just to Fred Franz and Nathan Knorr.

So what made a person eligible to serve on the Club's GB? He had to be one of the 144,000 and in good standing with the Club. A core doctrine of the Club is that only 144,000 human beings go to heaven after they die. JWs believe that God plans to restore the earth to a paradise after Armageddon, and it is on this paradise earth where most God-fearing people will live forever. Interestingly, Jesus and the 144,000 angels, all located in heaven, are expected to rule over everyone on the earth. Frankly, no one has ever explained to me why 144,000 rulers from heaven will be needed to rule over a perfect paradise world of God-loving people. What will they do?

What makes the 144,000 story an even bigger stretch is that key aspects of this doctrine were invented by Knorr's predecessor, Judge Rutherford. He taught in the mid-1930s that God stopped inviting the people He wanted to come to heaven. He closed the gate. If a person didn't live before 1914, and he or she turned out to be God-fearing, they would be resurrected and live forever on a paradise earth after they died.

I mention all of this so the reader gets an idea of how the Governing Body is compiled. Remember, to be appointed as a GB member, the man has to be one of the 144,000. So the seventeen men who served on the first GB were all senior citizens. [A side note: Mama told me that Knorr joined that elite group of 144,000 in heaven a millisecond after he died in June 1977.]

But what about the schism that formed after God anointed the Governing Body in 1976? For those who would like a detailed description of how it all started, played out, and went down, read Ray Franz's excellent eyewitness account in his book, *Crisis of Conscience*, published by Commentary Press 2002.

While Ray served competently on the Club's GB, he found something lacking in his life. He started reading his Bible far more intently than he had ever done before. He didn't read it with a *Watchtower* publication to tell him how to interpret things. He read it with an open mind. He encouraged others to do the same and to do it in small groups, praying for understanding. Soon, he and hundreds of other Bethelites began to question the Club's policy on several points, including the 144,000, 607 BC as a Bible-based date, and blood transfusions. To Ray's credit, he brought his concerns to GB meetings. Doing his homework, he could be very convincing. But like most religious groups at the governance level, change takes place very slowly.

While other members of the Governing Body jockeyed for position, Ray took his message to the rank-and-file at Bethel and to several key Club members around the world. He could see that many of the Club's sacred beliefs were not taught in the Bible. Ray encouraged open-minded people to start reading it. Many small groups formed and were energized by their studies. One did not have to have a *Watchtower* publication to make sense of the Bible.

Ray continued to express his concerns at GB meetings where he was asked to share his detailed research and interpretations. He recommended that several long-held doctrines of the Club be changed. He received over sixty percent support from fellow GB members when he asked them to repudiate the blood transfusion policy and the 144,000 doctrine. Unfortunately, before the Governing Body was formed, then-President Knorr insisted that it take a seventy-five percent consensus to change a Club doctrine. So each time Ray's recommendations came up for a vote, no change could be made. But it didn't stop Ray's efforts to correct what he believed to be genuine errors on the part of the Watchtower Society.

Ray wrote many years later about this difficult time in his life, "I had spent nearly forty years...serving at every level of the organizational structure. It was those final years that were the crucial period for me. Illusions there met up with reality. I have since come to appreciate [that] 'the great enemy of the truth is very often not the lie—deliberate, contrived dishonest—but the myth—persistent, persuasive and unrealistic.' I now began to realize how large a measure of what I had based my entire adult life course on was just that, a myth—persistent, persuasive and unrealistic."

Ray Franz Called it a Myth, I Call it the Ghost of Misinformation

The Governing Body eventually reached consensus on one key point: Ray Franz's questioning of the Club's core doctrines had to be stopped and Ray needed to be framed as a man who no longer loved Jehovah. He had to be disfellowshipped along with hundreds of Bethelites who supported him. And to make that possible, the GB reached the needed consensus to enact a new policy they called *shunning*, a policy that would be positioned as a new truth from Jehovah God.

The Ghost of Separation Uses Shunning Very Effectively

Before the new policy was announced to the rank-and-file members, all group study of the Bible was banned at Bethel. If a Bethelite was caught reading the Bible without a *Watchtower* publication, he would be dismissed and could be disfellowshipped. On April 30, 1980, Karl Klein, a member of the GB, summed it up

133

this way when he addressed the Bethel family members, "If you have a tendency towards *apostasy*, get a hobby and keep yourself busy to keep your mind off of it. *Stay away from deep Bible study to determine the meanings of scriptures.*"

The new policy on shunning was first announced in the September 15, 1981 issue of *The Watchtower*. It stated that Club members could no longer greet, say hello or share a meal with anyone who had been disfellowshipped or who had voluntarily dissociated from the Club. The disfellowshipped or dissociated person was to be treated as if he or she did not exist. In other words, he or she was to be *shunned*. And what would happen if a JW didn't follow this new truth from Jehovah God? He or she would die at Armageddon along with all nonbelievers.

You're Going to Die at Armageddon Unless…

In an effort at comfort and support, the Club provided the following caveat: "Naturally, if a close relative is disfellowshipped, human emotions can pose a major test for us. Sentiment and family ties are particularly strong between parents and their children, and they are also powerful when a marriage mate is disfellowshipped. Still, we must recognize that, in the final analysis, we will not benefit anyone or please God if we allow emotion to lead us into ignoring His wise counsel and guidance. We need to display our complete confidence in the perfect righteousness of God's ways, including His provision to disfellowship unrepentant wrongdoers. If we remain loyal to God and the congregation, the wrongdoer may in time take a lesson from that, repent, and be reinstated in the congregation. Yet, whether that occurs or not, we can draw comfort and strength from what David said late in life, '...And let Jehovah repay me according to my righteousness, according to my cleanness in front of His eyes. With someone loyal you will act in loyalty; with the faultless, mighty one, you will deal faultlessly; with the one keeping clean, you will show yourself clean... And the humble people you will save.' —2 Sam.22: 23-28."

This newly-revealed truth, purported to be directly from Jehovah God, would throw my world into total disarray, having disastrous consequences for my marriage with Helen.

Ray Franz was disfellowshipped in November1981and shunned by JWs until his death in 2010. What were the scriptural grounds? He was seen eating a meal with a disfellowshipped person. God's executioners did not consult with him or allow a rebuttal. They labeled Ray and told everyone that he had stopped loving Jehovah God. Ray Franz, a fallen angel, brought condemnation upon himself, now an apostate and unfit to speak to.

What makes this story even more bizarre is that when Ray served on the GB, he claimed to be one of the 144,000. Once he was disfellowshipped, JWs believed that God withdrew His offer to Ray of heavenly life. One is expected to believe that Jehovah then chose a younger man to receive the heavenly calling to become one of the 144,000. [So if it happened during the night, the new appointee would wake up in the morning and tell his wife, "I just got the heavenly calling from God. Whoopee, I'm one of the 144,000."]

Shunning
Chapter 19

The Ghost of Separation at Work on the Person Doing the Shunning

The Impact of Being Shunned

When I was *disfellowshipped* in 1977, I thought of it as a badge of honor and felt very proud of it. Yes, I had made a big mistake to earn that honor, but no one could any longer call me a JW just because my parents raised me as one. Three months after earning that title, I reconciled my marriage with Helen and it worked well for three-and-half years, in spite of religious differences. And JWs treated me kindly.

In 1981Clipper business hit at an all-time high, the MATO joint venture adding four million dollars of additional revenue. In August, the company moved its operations into in a new 105,000-square-foot, state-of the-art manufacturing facility that I and key employees helped design.

In September 1981, Helen, Keith, Kim and I looked forward to a four-day visit by my parents at our Grand Rapids home. Mama had stopped trying to get me back into the Club. I now experienced a mellower, *let's enjoy the life we've been given in this lifetime* side of my parents. But then Mama received the September 15 issue of *The Watchtower* in the mail.

I will never know what went through her mind or the minds of millions of JWs around the world when they read the official epistle from the Club. To go abruptly from a tolerant view of disfellowshipped or disassociated family members to a very severe you-must-shun-them position had to be an emotional jolt. Of course Club members were led to believe that the Creator of the Universe in His infinite wisdom had issued this new edict. No one dared ask, "Just what precipitated this [childish] mandate? Isn't this what uneducated, socially inept adolescents, bigots and racists would do?" It would be many years later before people learned that it was all about Ray Franz—a man I personally knew, a man who truly cared for his fellow human beings. Ray wouldn't hurt a flea and yet he dared to tell the Emperor that he was wearing no clothes.

I could go on and on about the injustices of many religious practices that play out differently and seldom positively in the lives of the people who choose to believe their church leaders have a direct link to God. And so it is with what is now my story.

Mama did not call me when she received the notice of God's change of mind. She called Helen instead, whom she never talked to on the phone. She said they couldn't come for the planned September visit at our home. She referred to *the new truth* in the

138

September 15 *Watchtower* as her reason. Helen hadn't read the article and asked what it was all about. Mama gave Helen the condensed version and Helen gasped. She wanted to know why it applied to me. Mama explained that in the eyes of God, I was still a fornicator. I had not gone to the local elders to petition for God's forgiveness. [Unless I went through a rigorous six-month *I fucked up my life but now I want to love Jehovah and worship alongside other Jehovah lovers*, I was still fucked, and no one could talk to me.] I would be shunned until I repented. This was God's way of making sure He didn't have to destroy me at Armageddon.

The Ghost of Misinformation Reporting that You're Going to Die Unless...

Helen told me about her conversation with Mama and asked me to read *The Watchtower* article. She thought this would help me see the wisdom of God's new position. I went ballistic with, "Fuck, no! You want me to look at a fucking gun that was used to obliterate my marriage. Helen, you're not thinking right. This is wrong and there has been a big misunderstanding."

I then called Mama. The tone in her voice answering the phone was ice cold. "Mama, this is Dick." No response, but I persevered. "Helen tells me that you cancelled your visit because of an article you read in *The Watchtower*. Can you tell me what it's all about?"

"Dick, it's hard for me to talk about it. I think it would be better if you read it for yourself."

"So why aren't you coming? What would you like me to tell the kids?

"Dick, it was you who left Helen for another woman. You brought this upon yourself."

"Listen, what happened with Helen and me is between Helen and me. She has forgiven me. And besides, you are talking about something that happened almost four years ago. I made a mistake, an error in judgment. Now is now. You seemed to be able to accept me six months ago."

"This is Jehovah's way of getting you back in The Truth. Can't you see His love in this policy? I do."

"Mama, you are an asshole." She hung up.

Beside myself for the next thirty minutes, I decided to call my brother Tim. He answered on the second ring. "Tim, this is your brother Dick. I think there's been a mistake. Can we talk?"

Tim's response was icier than Mama's, "No, and it's because you're a fornicator."

I hung up immediately. As bizarre as all this was, it was real. And I would have to deal with it. Unfortunately, Helen could not help me. When people are trapped in a cult because they want to please their mother and friends who are members of the same cult, it creates a monster conundrum. And all of this is the work of misinformation, the most formidable of the Ghosts from Mama's Club.

The Hauntingly Horrible Ghost of Misinformation

When I came home from work the next day, Helen told me that she had talked with Mama on the phone. My parents had decided to make the visit to Grand Rapids as planned. But they would stay in a motel. From there, my parents could visit with

Helen, Keith and Kim. They would get a motel with an indoor pool so the kids could swim during their visit.

"So Helen, you would do that? You would sanction a policy where it would be okay to shun me for something I did four years ago?"

"Yes, I don't see anything wrong with that. You have to remember that you brought this upon yourself, not me."

I did not raise my voice and I did not use vulgar language, although I chose my words wisely. "Helen, I don't think you're thinking straight at the moment. Hopefully, you'll see it all clearly when the dust settles. But if I were to put myself in your shoes, I could not do what you are suggesting. We are a family and we will stick together as a family. If you'd like to see my parents on your own, you can do that. But you will not take my children."

"No, I don't want to see them. I was just thinking about the kids."

"Helen, this is not up for a vote. I'm going to call my mother and tell her that she's not welcome anywhere near our home. If she's not going to speak to me, she's not going to speak to the kids."

"Dick, it's your decision and I will stand with you on this one. But I have to talk with one of the elders. I need some advice."

It's ironic that she chose to meet and talk with John Meulenberg, a JW Elder, and now the VP of Clipper. His advice to Helen: "There's been a big mistake here. Dick should not be treated this way. Just give it some time and I know that Jehovah will correct this injustice."

More aftershocks from the new shunning policy took place three weeks later when five JW Clipper employees quit their jobs. They had been told by the Club's hierarchy to find other jobs. John did not take their advice, and two years later dissociated himself from the Club. While the shunning issue wasn't the straw that broke the camel's back, it was a weighty one and it helped him see the light—that the Club is a high-control, dangerous cult, led by a group of old, delusional men.

While I recognized the man-made nature of the shunning policy, that did little to combat the emotional pain it inflicted. It was as if twenty-three family members all died in the same plane crash and there were no funeral services. The most difficult part was that Helen could not see it. We would be having dinner somewhere and a Club member would come over to the table and greet Helen, acting like I didn't exist. JWs would come to our home and if I was there, they'd treat me like wallpaper or the invisible man. It was a challenge to keep my cool, although at times I went off on Helen for being so insensitive. While I tried to use good logic, she always seemed confused that the act of being shunned bothered me. This was a definite blind spot for Helen.

Helen's mother performed at her all-time worst during this period. Not only would she *not* greet me in a civil way, but she chose to come to the house when I was not around to boost Helen's spirits, telling her that she would be better off if she divorced me.

Kim, who had recently stopped going to the meetings with her mom, happened to walk in on one of those conversations. She entered the house from the garage and walked into the kitchen where Grandma Geerling was giving Helen an earful.

When Gertrude saw Kim, she seized on the opportunity to pump her granddaughter up with some Gertrude guilt, but first she needed to prime the well. "Why, Kim, it's nice to see you. I have something for you." Then she gave Kim a clean, crisp twenty-dollar bill.

Kim had the money in her hand and was about to thank her grandma, when Gertrude abruptly said, "Kim, I want you to know I'm very disappointed in you. I hear you've stopped going to the meetings. Not good! Your mom needs your support during these trying times. Armageddon is very close."

Gertrude Guilt, It Don't Get Better Than That

Kim looked at her mom, thinking she would get some support. Unfortunately, Helen didn't say a thing. Finally, Kim spoke up. But first, she threw the twenty-dollar bill back at her grandma. "Here, you take it. I don't want your bribe money."

It would be the last conversation, if that's what you can call it, that Kim and her Grandma Geerling would ever have together. Kim also never again went to a meeting at the Kingdom Hall, with or without her mother.

Shunning is an awful, inhumane policy. It does as much damage to the person doing the shunning as it does to the person being shunned. Eventually Helen would see the harm it created for our family and how senseless it had been. Since 1981, over one million JWs have abandoned the Club, in large part because of the Club's shunning policy.

It is now 2012 and my brother, Tim, and his wife, Esther, have shunned me for over thirty years. If I walked by them in the street, they would turn the other way and pretend I didn't exist. Does it hurt? Yes, but the wounds heal and you replace biological family with adopted family, friends who share your values, care for you unconditionally, love to laugh, share common interests, and enjoy their lives. It also helps if you enjoy your work life.

Before sharing how Helen and I resolved the shunning problems and more, I would like to jump forward in time. To take the reader from what was for me the worst of times to the best of times. And the next two chapters were definitely *the best of times*.

Saying Goodbye to Clipper
Chapter 20

While my wife, children, grandchildren and some very good friends, come first in my life, I cannot imagine what life would have been without Clipper Belt Lacer Company. For all the years that I worked at Clipper, I daily enjoyed the good honest work that focused on creating value for the customer, not on how much money we could make. The products we made helped make the world a better, safer place to live. How many people can say that about their life's work?

In May 1995, I sold my shares in the company and stepped down as the company's president, an employee for nearly thirty years. While it marked the end of my personal work-life journey, I could not have been more pleased with what had been accomplished under my watch. Sales and profits were at all-time highs. The company had instituted state-of-the-art manufacturing processes. We were designing new and improved products in a modern office and factory. Well-educated employees were empowered to make decisions to improve their work processes. A company-wide suggestion system encouraged all employees to continually eliminate waste. And the State of Michigan showered the company with accolades for our system of continuous improvement.

What I'm most proud of during my tenure at Clipper was raising the bar of manufacturing excellence. In 1989, I decided the company had the potential to be a world-class manufacturer, knowing it was not an easy task to change a company's culture. I believed it to be an imperative strategy, as we had just parted ways with our German joint-venture partner. We needed to attract a new, dynamic, marketing-oriented company. If we excelled in making things, it would be a good match.

My plan was to model our company after Toyota, who had used Ed Deming's Total Quality Management (TQM) principles to produce better cars at lower prices than American manufacturers in a relatively short period of time. (*Out of the Crisis* by W. Edwards Deming, 1986)

TQM functions on the premise that the quality of products and processes is the responsibility of everyone involved in the creation and consumption of the products and services an organization offers. TQM capitalizes on the involvement of management, workforce, suppliers, and even customers, in order to meet or exceed customer expectations.

Clipper's TQM would start at the top. All employees, including me, were required to take an inventory of their personal strengths and weaknesses, and to make a commitment to improve. Not everyone could do it. Some ill feelings developed and some employees went to work for other companies. But radical cultural change required everyone to get on board, and this eventually happened.

We taught every employee how to diagram the work processes they were responsible for and how it could be measured. All employees identified the users of or *customers* for their individual and department outputs. We asked our internal and external customers what we could do to make the products or services we created better. We then eliminated those things that didn't create value for them.

We encouraged employees to suggest ways to eliminate waste in their areas of responsibility. Eventually we made it mandatory for every employee to submit six suggestions a year, counting only implemented ones. A scoreboard with measurable goals for quality, cost, delivery, employee involvement and safety were set up in each department. The financial department contributed their skills to generate monthly data for these boards, which was used to set department and corporate strategies.

Late in 1994, I led a tour of Clipper's factory and office for Mick Ramsey and Rick White of Flexible Steel Lacing Company (Flexco). I felt like a proud father showing off his kids. What a dramatic difference from the company that employed me in 1965. Most of the manufacturing was now done in work cells. Cleanliness, order and smooth workflow were trademarks for all departments. Employees knew their roles and how to measure their own and the company's success on easy-to-read scoreboards.

Shortly after that visit, Flexco made several offers to buy the company before a purchase price was agreed upon. It was a good business match for sure, as Flexco had excellent marketing skills and good distribution channels. Today, the Flexco Grand Rapids operation is going strong, known around the world for its manufacturing excellence.

When you have been happy doing what you have done for many years, there's always going to be a feeling of loss when you retire. So it was for me. But getting to see the world and doing it with your wife, adult children, granddaughters and good friends in places like Tuscany, I got over it quickly.

John Meulenberg, who you may recall I hired in 1971, still works for Flexco Grand Rapids and he and the company are doing very well. Some of the manufacturing work processes in his world-class factory are lights out. And John's critical thinking skills see the light of day, every day, now that he is no longer a member of the Club, twenty-seven years and counting. In 2011, he met the love of his life, a soulmate, Stephanie McNamara.

Sharing the Good Times in Tuscany
Chapter 21

I began this book, my story, with our trip to Tuscany in 2006. While I will not end it here, I would like to revisit what may have been the best vacation I have ever had. It's where this book, *The Ghosts from Mama's Club*, was conceived; yes, in Tuscany, the birthplace of the Renaissance.

During our stay at Villa Casa Bianca, we decided to save the empty wine bottles, inventorying them on the inner edge of a concrete, horseshoe-shaped bar that we called the Circle of Shame. We had our evening meals and happy hours seated around this cement table as its location provided the best view of the long, wide Pesa Valley far below and the nightly setting of the Tuscan sun.

The afternoon before our son Keith, his wife Amy, and the twins, Hannah and Katrina, were to leave for their Texas home, we had a population explosion at the villa. Along with Kim's family of four, Helen and I were joined by our Tucson La Paloma neighbors and friends, Don and Cheryl Brown, and Tom and Jen Hall from Grand Rapids. That evening all of us were seated around the Circle of Shame singing John Prine and Todd Snider songs. Because the lyrics are so detailed and lengthy, we'd get lost at times. Fortunately, my ten-year-old granddaughter, Katrina, remembered every word. My head fills with melody and joy as I remember that impromptu group singalong in one of the most beautiful places in the world.

I also fondly remember reading a letter that Katrina's sister, Hannah, stuffed in my pocket as she readied herself to leave. It read: "Dear Nana and Poppa, Thanks for making this trip to Italy the highlight of my summer. It was sooooooo fun. I hope to do it again sometime. I will miss you something awful. But I am sure you will all have another great week in Italy. Thanks again for one of the best trips of a lifetime. Thanks a lot." Signed, Hannah K.

For me, that letter from my ten-year-old granddaughter sums up the trip's success. It's always a pleasure to see the fruits of good parenting. I would like to say that letter is as good as it gets, but something that happened on Friday, July 7, the last full day at the villa, may have topped it.

Our villa host, Franco Grossi, told me about me about a spectacular outdoor Tuscany restaurant experience that we should not miss. So we planned to spend lunchtime and the afternoon in Rignana of Chianti, at Ristorante La Cantinetta di Rignana. There would be ten people at the Ristorante: Steve and Milagros Lassos, Dean and Norine Kasten, Don and Cheryl Brown, Darrell Miller, Bob Mihallik, Helen and me.

Steve and I grew up as Jehovah's Witnesses. We have been lifetime friends from when we first met at eight years of age. He left the Club the same time that I did. Millie is Helen's clone, and people aren't happier or more joyful to be around than Milagros. Dean, like Helen, is a twin and if you don't like him, it's your problem. He and Norine grew up as JWs but left the Club years ago. I met Cheryl while walking the golf course at our La Paloma home in Tucson. Don is a city manager by trade, but now retired. When Don was courting Cheryl, he thought she was the smartest person he'd ever met. For me, that honor goes to Darrell. We met Darrell and his partner Bob at a Tucson wine dinner. They were retired snowbirds who cultivated friendships like gardeners nurturing prize-winning plants and flowers.

Imagine the ten of us, sequestered on a high Chianti ridge, in one of the most remote parts of Tuscany, seated outdoors and doted on by a five-star wait staff on a drop-dead-blue-sky day. I don't remember having communion with a more animated, happy and appreciative group of friends, soulmates partaking of Paul-Bunyan portions of truffles, decadent, Italian-style cheeses and meats, and deep-red Tuscan wine produced from the Sangiovese grape vineyards surrounding the Ristorante.

It was a very special day for me, one that I will never forget—the best meal that I have ever had. Why? It could have been the food, maybe the wine, the wait staff the postcard landscape, the perfect temperature, the rich blue sky, or the rays from the Tuscan sun. Well, it was all of that. But what made it so memorable is that it was a shared experience with adopted brothers and sisters, real friends, people who thoroughly enjoy the life they've been blessed with, the life that they have *now*, not the one that the Club promises them if. . .

Should Helen and I have been willing to give up our life for the adopted brothers and sisters we shared that special Tuscan meal with at the Rignana Ristorante? You decide after reading the next chapter.

Helen, Bente & 1986
Chapter 22

The Club's new policy on shunning had been in effect for a year in the fall of 1982. A deeply flawed theological doctrine, it had a significant impact on my life. I could learn to live with family and friends who think it's Godlike to ignore me, to pretend I don't exist. But when my wife—who will talk with me—thinks it's an okay policy that JW family and friends need to shun me to stay right with God, I have a problem with that. Could I just be feeling sorry for myself?

Knowing for a year that Helen couldn't see how harmful shunning was for me and our family, I had second thoughts about staying in the marriage. I loved her, but I didn't know how long I could go on living with this burden. At times my stomach wrenched and head spun so that I thought I might be having a nervous breakdown, of all people me: strong, healthy, independent and able to think for myself. Why couldn't I just say no to my shunning anxieties and be done with it? Maybe a shrink could help me. But the really hard part was seeing Helen oblivious to the fact that it pained me. She seemed to think that it was okay for fellow JWs to treat me this way. After all, I brought this on myself.

When she went to the Kingdom Hall or in the door-to-door work, I saw these acts as disgusting. How could she party with the enemy? One JW Clipper employee couldn't find comparable work, so couldn't quit his job; but he refused to speak to me. Several JWs, employees of Clipper suppliers, would turn their heads when I passed them in the hallway at work. I would see long letters from Helen's JW sister, and it didn't take a brain surgeon to figure what she wrote about. We would be eating at a restaurant and one of Helen's JW friends would walk up to the table and talk with her, pretending I didn't exist. Watching Helen talking with them like this intrusion was okay hurt me, and every time it happened I would get this sharp pain in my stomach.

After being shunned for several months, I thought about writing an editorial for the Grand Rapids Press. I could expose how the Club really operates, destroying families recklessly in the name of God and love. If I did a good job, maybe I could bring down the Club, smash the Watchtower at its foundation. My sweet fantasy, but it wasn't realistic. There will always be people who want to buy into high-control religion. I needed to use my time more constructively.

The Ghost of Indignation Trying to Get Me to Topple the Club

Fortunately, after a year of shunning, Helen started to question the Christ-like nature of this behavior. The Club had been wrong many times in the past. Getting new light and repudiating one-time-sacred Club beliefs and policies was an annual event for JWs. This had to be one of those doctrines that would die a natural death, maybe next year at an assembly. In the meantime, she took the matter to Jehovah, knowing He would fix it in His good time. But she could no longer be insensitive to me. It also helped that I buried myself in my work, jogged every day and played my fair share of softball or basketball. However, intimacy, in hibernation for a year, began to slowly see the light of day.

Good things come to those who wait. At least that's how it played out for Helen and me. From the fall of 1982 until January 1986, Helen began to dial down her commitment, this need to go to every meeting at the Kingdom Hall and to go door-to-door every week. She still believed that we were living in the last days, that Armageddon and the New World were Bible-based, but she began to slowly "fall out of the Truth," per Helen's assessment.

She knows *the exact straw* that broke the camel's back, and the time place that it happened. She was attending the 1:00 PM Sunday Public Talk at the Grandville Kingdom Hall in January 1986. The speaker was a man we both knew very well. We used to party and go dancing with him and his wife at local honky-tonk bars in Grand Rapids. He had also tried to convince me to come back into the fold, to love Jehovah just as he did, to go to the meetings and knock on doors. It was 1974 and he said that it wasn't too late to become a Jehovah lover. The world would be destroyed in 1975 and like the prodigal son, I could be saved and live forever in God's New World if I changed my mind and ways. When I declined, he begged me again to come back. If I did and Armageddon didn't occur in 1975, he would leave the Club with me on January 1, 1976. I laughed and said "no" again.

He was up giving a one-hour-public talk. Halfway into it, he asked everyone in the audience to look at the person sitting to their right and the person to their left. "Take a good long look at them," he advised. "These are your brothers and sisters, real brothers and sisters in the faith. Each of you should be able to give up your life for them."

Helen thought to herself, "This guy would no more give up his life up for me or anyone else. This is bull shit. Why am I sitting here?"

Helen stayed in her seat while the Public Talk droned on. But she decided in that chair, in that moment: The Club does not have the truth. I am going to walk out of this Hall after this meeting and I will never come back. And in fact, that is exactly what happened. She did not attend the Watchtower Study meeting, which she would have normally done. To Helen's credit and good fortune, she would never be haunted with any of the ghosts from Mama's Club.

When she came home from the meeting early and told me what had happened, I was stunned by the news. But I knew that's how Helen often made decisions. She would have no trouble leaving the Club, or assimilating into mainstream society.

Unlike Many Ex-JWs, Helen had No Problem Assimilating into Mainstream Society

In fact, Helen embraced her new freedom. At the time, we knew Kim would enroll at Michigan State University in the fall. Keith, a student at Michigan Tech for two years, was working on a degree in chemical engineering. Helen and I would soon be empty-nesters. With two empty bedrooms looming, Helen chose to fill that void by having an exchange student live with us for nine months.

A neighborhood friend, Judy Campbell, headed the exchange-student program and provided us with a brochure of students to choose from. A resume from a young lady in Kongsberg, Norway, stood out, a good fit for our family. So Helen and I invited Bente Skalstad to come live with us and attend the 12th grade at Wyoming Park High School.

We picked Bente up at the Grand Rapids airport early in September, an exciting delivery for us. When I first saw Bente walk out of the plane's gateway, I recognized her immediately. She looked exactly as I had pictured her in the brochures. But her knees shook as if gripped with palsy, the finality of her nine-month commitment suddenly overwhelming her. After we hugged and introduced ourselves, Bente relaxed and talking came easy for her.

After a week, we knew Bente's life story. She was a Daddy's girl and a tomboy with a mind of her own. She'd been spoiled sufficiently but not excessively, and was very smart. Self-disciplined, attuned to world events, she had excellent study habits and picked friends with good values.

Bente's uncle in Norway had married and divorced a JW, so she knew about the Club and its policy on shunning. We openly talked about Mama, who had not spoken to me in over five years.

On a Saturday late in October, the phone rang. I walked into the bedroom, picked it up and said hello. To my great surprise, I heard Mama's voice. "Hello Dickie, this is your mom. How are you?"

I gasped and choked up, feeling dizzy. Was I having a panic attack? Not sure what my body was telling me, I sat on the bed. Finally, with some hesitation I mustered a response, "I'm doing fine. But I thought you weren't allowed to talk with me."

Mama did not answer my question. "Dickie, Dad and I are planning to visit with Aunt Norma at her new home in the Sierra Nevada Mountains, a hundred miles east of Sacramento. We were wondering if you and Helen would like to join us for three days."

My head swirled with the offer, a chance to talk with Mama after five years without a word. Norma was Mama's sister and not a JW, and would never be one. Even though Norma had been adamant about it, Mama still visited with her from time to time. I thought about asking if her sister knew she hadn't spoken to me for over five years, but quickly discarded the idea.

"Mom, thanks for calling, but I couldn't do something like

157

that. I hope everything's all right, but I have to go."

My heart pounded. I felt as nerved up as I can ever recall feeling. Did what just happened, really happen? I thought for a moment and knew Mama could be a Jekyll and Hyde if she didn't think other JWs would find out what she was up to. Then it hit me—maybe I had just lost a mother and at the same time, gained a daughter. This proved to be true, for both me and Helen.

In December, Helen's sister Ellie Kleinheksel called to tell us that that their mother, Gertrude, was dying in the hospital. Surgery had not gone well and she would soon bleed to death. A blood transfusion would save her life, but Gertrude vehemently protested. Ellie told the doctor to honor those wishes. She had only a few hours to live and Gertrude wanted to see Helen before she died. The two of them had not spoken for ten months—ever since Helen left the Club.

Helen told Ellie she didn't want to see her mom, then she hung up. In Bente's presence, I tried to persuade her to go. It was the right thing to do, a time and place to bring closure. She would never get another chance. Her mom had been a good mom while she was growing up. Fortunately, Helen did go and say goodbye. Gertrude died peacefully with Helen and Ellie by her side. But not before Gertrude asked her daughters to do what it would take so that they would be with her in paradise. She wanted to see her girls after being resurrected and then for all of them to live forever in a righteous new world.

Funeral arrangements were made and I knew that it would be the proper thing for Helen, me, Kim and Bente to go to the visitation and the funeral. Keith could not attend because Houghton and the Upper Peninsula were snowed in that weekend. Bente did not want to go at first. I reminded her that we were a family now, she was a part of that family, and I wanted her to experience the good and the bad that comes with being part of a family, our family. Like so many times, when one took the time to explain something logically to Bente, she always made the right decision.

Bente went back home to Norway in July 1987 and one year later, her father, Hans Skalstad, died. His enlarged heart erupted while riding a bicycle with her brother, Roar. He was forty-four and in the prime of his life. While I have never attempted to replace him—it wasn't possible—I wanted to be there when and if she needed my help. And so it happened.

Helen and I have treated and loved Bente as our own daughter; she is our daughter, since she first came to live with us as an exchange student. She has always made good choices, and her husband, Harald Rishovd, was one of her best. Today, Bente's mother, Inger, and Harald's mother, Gro, are part of our extended family. And two of the best gifts that Bente and Harald have given to Helen and me are two beautiful, vibrant and sometimes mischievous granddaughters. Ingvild is now thirteen and Silje is eleven, going on eighteen.

Our life would not be what it is without Bente and her family. When an opportunity knocked on our door after the Club instituted its shunning policy, we opened it.

What has given Helen angst over the last twenty-five years is that she finds it difficult to imagine why she didn't see the light sooner. How could she have done those painful things? Still a bit challenged by why she stayed a JW for so many years, I remind her of the power of brainwashing, how it oppresses and destroys a person's critical thinking skills. The ghosts of separation and dependency also played a significant role in keeping her in the dark for so long.

Today many of Helen's friends have a hard time imagining that she could have once been a JW. Helen's biggest concern when I told her that I wanted to write *The Ghosts from Mama's Club* was, "What will people think about me when they learn what I did in the name of religion? They'll think I'm a nutcase." But I assured her that readers will judge her fairly. I believe people will be inspired by what she has accomplished. In my mind, the hero in this story is my wife, Helen Joan Kelly.

However, this book is dedicated to my sister, Marilyn Faye Kelly, and it is now time to tell *her* story.

Marilyn's Story
Part One
Chapter 23

My sister, Marilyn Faye Kelly, was born on September 17, 1948. Her conception had been a gift from Mama to thank Papa for capitulating to her wishes that he convert. Papa had fought valiantly for two months trying to keep Mama from joining the Club. But when he realized how fruitless it would be, he decided to join her. Marilyn was the physical evidence, the living proof, of that capitulation.

Babies don't get more beautiful than Marilyn, what with her thick blond hair, sparkling blue-green eyes and engaging smile. When my parents brought her home from the hospital, I, nearly five, knew she was special. When she turned five, she could pass for a human Barbie doll with her soft, pink-white skin sprinkled with fairy-dust freckles. For sure Mama loved her, but Marilyn was Daddy's Girl. I think Papa took it personally that he helped produce such a beautiful child.

Marilyn made few demands on her parents. Everyone liked her, and those big beautiful eyes and vibrant blond hair made it easy for people to remember her name, little Marilyn Monroe. She also didn't cry constantly as our sister Susan did. She easily entertained herself and didn't require lots of work. She had a very submissive nature, which made her easy for Mama to manipulate and mold. Unfortunately, Marilyn lacked the innate sense of curiosity that most kids possess; but that would come into play later.

As a teenager, Marilyn didn't have my blemish problems, a bumper crop of pimples and blackheads to boot. She had no symptoms of bosom-envy cocooning into womanhood. Breast implants would play no role in her life. Mama kept the boys at bay with heavy doses of guilt so Marilyn's hormones didn't have a chance to make a single bad decision.

But she had a significant handicap. Abe Lincoln would have called it *the slows*. It took Marilyn forever to do what she had to do or to get to where she wanted to go. While she was definitely a very attractive woman, that too would turn out to be a handicap for her.

Marilyn learned and easily accepted the fact that girls were second-class citizens in the eyes of Jehovah God. Surely Mama schooled her with some version of this: "Jehovah loves all of His earthly children just the same. But He's persnickety about protocol. All living creatures have their place in His hierarchy. First there is Jesus and then the angels. Below them are men. Next in the pecking order are women. Below women are animals. And, if one doesn't want to anger God, no one should dare challenge his or her place in His grand scheme of things."

Even as a child, I'd translate Mama's beliefs like that. It would make her so angry. Mama would yell at me, telling me to stop, warning me of the dangerous ground on which I trod.

I wish I could have told Mama what I know today about women. In Jesus' time, they were treated like chattel. The Jewish religion supported that view: according to the book of Genesis, women were created by God solely for the purpose of serving man as a helpmate (Genesis 2:18). Later in the Ten Commandments, building on this sense of second-class citizenship, women were defined as property (Exodus 20:17). Thus polygamy made sense, for a man could have as many wives, sheep, or cattle as he could afford.

In stark contrast, Jesus was non-sexist. He tried to end discrimination of women. He had female disciples. He traveled and ministered with them. He treated women as equals, breaking the religious rules of his day. But that all changed after Jesus died. The Christian church went back to the sexist mentality of the Old Testament.

For much of Western history, women were relegated to second-class status, with many Christian orthodox churches validating that definition as God-inspired and God-imposed. A woman's lack of size, speed and physical strength was used to relegate her to a state of childlike dependency. In the most basic relationship in human society, the male met his survival needs by claiming that the female's lower status was God's plan in creation. That way if the woman objected, she had to fight against God as well.

I would have liked to share those kinds of thoughts with Mama and ask her, "Was the discrimination of women an invention of God or man? Could it be that a select group of men created God in their image?" But in the end, she would plod forward with her version of *the truth*, blind to the damage her beliefs inflicted on Marilyn.

To make matters worse, my parents didn't encourage Marilyn to get an education. If Armageddon didn't show up before her time to marry, Marilyn could find a smart guy in good standing with the Club. He would be the breadwinner and take care of her, as Papa had done for Mama. Marilyn did not need to excel in school. Though smart enough, she was not encouraged to develop her thinking skills.

Marilyn had no close friends as a child. Perhaps there were kids at school that she met and liked, but Mama would have treated them like lepers. Worldly kids would get her into trouble. So Marilyn didn't develop the social skills that she would need as an adult. Not a big concern for Mama, as she knew the end of this old world loomed just around the corner. A new paradisiacal world, in their lifetime, would resolve this deficiency.

I have no warm fuzzy anecdotes about our childhood to share, no sweet memories of big brother/little sister conversations, interesting games that we played, treasured walks that we took together. They came later in life, in dribbles as adults, but not as children. My role as a big brother focused on protection, which I managed to do several times. I also did my fair share of teasing.

We moved to Nebraska in 1958, and like all the homes we lived in while growing up, there was only one bathroom for our family of six. Marilyn took forever to do her business, so it could be a challenge when I had to go. One day I pounded on the door, pleading for her to finish so I wouldn't pee in my pants. Finally, she opened the door and walked out. I rushed in and opened the toilet lid. After a few minutes of boyish deliberation, I called her the "Little Logger." The name stuck until the day she died.

Shortly after Marilyn graduated from high school, she tried to find part-time work in Columbus. But without an advanced education, there weren't a lot of jobs available except for cleaning homes and offices. She tried that kind of work at several places, but her services would no longer be needed after a few days on the job. She never said it, but I knew why. Marilyn had the slows.

Marilyn lived at home for over two years and could not find work. Because she didn't help out financially, tension began to mount between Marilyn and our parents. Marilyn also resented the special treatment our mentally-handicapped sister, Susan, received, and she and Susan bickered constantly. Marilyn was desperate and decided she needed help.

It was 1969 and I had been an ex-JW for four years when she called me on the phone. Could she move to Grand Rapids? Could she live with us for the first two weeks? She wanted to find a job and a place to live. I talked it over with Helen and we told her yes. It would give us a chance to get to know her as an adult. However, only two days into her stay with us, Helen had her concerns. Marilyn helped around the house, but you had to ask her. Like Mama, when she visited, she preferred to be waited on. But to her credit, Marilyn didn't take offence when we told her she needed to take more initiative. Unfortunately, Marilyn still suffered from the slows.

Marilyn found a job working for a small Chinese restaurant in the north end of Grand Rapids, about fifteen miles from the house. Tim and Esther helped her find an apartment within walking distance of work and Marilyn started attending meetings at their Kingdom Hall. She began dating a young JW man and all seemed to be going well. Then she informed us that she planned to go back to Nebraska. She had lived away from home for four months, but she wasn't happy. She spent more money than she made and she didn't really like her work.

Six months later she called to tell me that she had met the man of her dreams in Nebraska. They were going to get married and she wanted Helen, me and the kids to attend the wedding. His name was Jerome Roper and he came from a big family of well-to-do JWs in central Nebraska. Everyone liked the Roper family. She didn't know what Jerome would do for work, but his parents would help him find a job. They would also pay the rent for their first house. The key ingredients for a responsible husband appeared to be missing. However, if Marilyn loved Jerome and he made her happy, why shouldn't I be happy for her?

Three months after they were married, Marilyn and Jerome came to visit us. Jerome, a carefree sort of guy, seemed disconnected from Marilyn. He hinted about staying in Grand Rapids if I could get him a job at Clipper. When I first met his brothers and dad, I had a feeling they had a good work ethic, but that's not how I sized up Jerome.

A day into their visit, he asked if some evening he and I could go to a strip bar. He assumed that because I wasn't a JW, I liked those kinds of worldly things. While I wanted to smack him, I played along, so he let me in on a little secret. He liked pornography. When I asked if Marilyn knew about it, he said yes. She didn't like it, but they were working on it.

The next day, I told Marilyn about my conversation with Jerome. She was pleased I had confided in her, but disappointed that I hadn't confronted and shamed his poor behavior. Stunned, I told Marilyn she had a problem on her hands. Nothing I could say or do to this guy would change him. He was a self-centered boy, disguised in a man's body. Leopards don't change their spots.

165

Marilyn had an even temperament, making it fairly easy to share bad news. She grabbed my hand and told me how grateful she was for our little talk. It turns out Jerome could also be a control freak and he had been abusive. Not physical stuff, but he could go off on verbal rants that made our handicapped sister's use of the f-word seem like child's play. They stayed with us for another day, went back to Nebraska and in less than a week, Marilyn annulled their marriage.

Two years later, in 1972, Marilyn reported to me of meeting the second man of her dreams, this time the guy was the real deal. While on a trip to Georgia, she met Mr. Wonderful, who she claimed to be an exemplary JW, although a recent convert. Ruggedly handsome, he doted on her and she loved it.

"Does he have any baggage?" I asked.

"Oh, he had a big drug problem while growing up and he hates his dad. But then he found the Truth. People tell me that he's a changed man. He's a workaholic whether working for a living or working for Jehovah."

Helen and I did not attend the wedding. But the two of them visited us shortly after getting married. Carter Wilcox bore no resemblance to Marilyn's first husband, intellectually or emotionally. He seemed totally devoted to her. They were truly in love. Carter was not a big talker but what he said made sense. He had some interesting ideas about how he could make money selling and servicing computers, a business-savvy guy.

On the other hand, he seemed difficult to like from a guy's standpoint, maybe a bit of a con. And he couldn't connect with Helen. Not a good sign. I also sensed Carter's unease about me not being a JW.

Marilyn and Carter bought a home in Columbus, Nebraska. To the best of my knowledge, they were a model JW couple, doing all the things that make JWs unique. Carter started and operated a successful computer business. They did well financially and started a family, a son and a daughter. But having kids didn't happen until after I was disfellowshipped and the Club's shunning policy was in place. So I never had a presence or place in their kids' lives. I did know that my parents never liked Carter. The feelings were mutual, but Carter took it to a much higher level of intensity. I have never seen anyone, except for Carter, turn *hate* into an art form.

I had had no communication with Marilyn for fourteen years. That, however, came to an abrupt halt when I received a surprise telephone call from her in the spring of 1991. It was strange and yet good to hear her voice. She couldn't apologize enough. She had waited way too long before she dared talk with me. She had heard that my 30-year high school reunion would be held in Columbus, in the summer and wondered if Helen and I were going. She hoped we would and she wanted to have a relationship with us. I hadn't planned to go, but decided immediately that I would open the door to this opportunity.

Marilyn also invited us to have dinner with her at her house. She and Carter were separated but the kids would be there. My parents and our sister Susan, all of whom I hadn't seen in over ten years, would also be there. I didn't say it, but this news was a huge red flag. Marilyn had to be in big trouble; this made no sense. If JWs had a meal with me, they would be disfellowshipped and shunned just like Ray Franz.

What had been dropped in Marilyn's lap? She acted like all was business as usual. She and Carter were separated, but that's all I knew. I had no idea of how *low* our brother Tim had stooped to uphold an inhumane policy. To tell this part of the story, I must go back in time and share events that precipitated Marilyn's phone call.

A Club policy that Carter seemed to cherish most is that men are allotted special privileges over women. A man is the head of his house, king of his home, regardless of his intellectual or emotional status. This gives him certain rights. If he wants to verbally abuse his wife, he can do so with immunity, as long as he does it with his wife's best interests in mind.

Early in their marriage, Carter had been verbally abusive to Marilyn, ratcheting it up ever so slowly as the years passed. Verbal abuse was not a new experience for Marilyn. Ironically, Mama had a talent for it and regularly performed her verbal magic on Papa for as long as I can remember. He tolerated it; so why couldn't Marilyn do the same? After all, Carter provided well for her physical needs, and he was a good JW.

However, three years before Marilyn called me, Carter physically abused her for the first time and that scared her. While he did not abuse her regularly, he was not averse to threats and she later learned that these bouts occurred shortly after he chug-a-lugged from a bottle of hard liquor he thought hidden in the basement.

He had been verbally abusive about Marilyn's spotty house-keeping, being late and getting on his nerves for no good reason early in their marriage. With the advent of children, his tirades increased. Marilyn handled constructive criticism well and I'm convinced that if Carter had picked his battles and not attacked Marilyn's self-esteem, it would have been a win-win. The bottom line is that no woman, no person, should be treated the way Marilyn was treated. What made Carter's abuse even worse was that around other JWs he acted like a perfect gentleman. He would go into his abusive rants only when the two of them were together or sometimes when the kids were around.

In an effort to get him to stop, she said that she planned to go to the elders at her Hall and report his abuses. But what made that strategy dicey was that our brother, Tim, served as one of those elders. Carter knew she would do it and he decided to help his cause. He asked to meet with Tim alone. He told Tim how delusional Marilyn could be, particularly since they had kids. Carter explained how any effort to help improve her parenting or housekeeping skills were met with the complaint, "You're abusing me."

Carter Wilcox wanted to stack the deck in his favor, and he did an effective job of painting Marilyn as a wacky woman. She needed Carter's leadership: Daddy Carter, the head of the family, needed to be in control and Marilyn was fighting it. Tim and Carter stood solid, convinced that a wife must allow her husband to pull her strings.

When Marilyn first met with the elders, she told them every-thing, her primary concern being the day-to-day verbal abuse. But he had physically hurt her several times. She believed that it wasn't beyond Carter after drinking too much and in a wild, frenzied state to kill her. The meeting continued for over an hour. Tim spoke first and suggested that she might be imagining some of this.

"What if he kills me? What happens then?"

"Marilyn, that isn't going to happen. If it should, you will always have the hope of a resurrection if you've been a loyal and faithful wife."

"So, what if I ask him to leave? I think a trial separation would help both of us."

Tim again responded with, "Marilyn, Carter is the head of your house. If he decides that's an appropriate response, so be it. But it will be his decision."

Exasperated by the meeting, Marilyn went home scared for her life. She knew Carter would learn about the meeting and the elders' recommendation. The next two weeks were a living hell. Carter took his abuse to a new level, threatening bodily harm if she went to the elders again. Marilyn's self-esteem slid to a new low. She tried praying, hoping Jehovah would intervene. It helped to talk to Mama, but Marilyn had been doing that for years. Mama had a standard pat response: "Let's just wait on Jehovah. He knows all and will take care of it in His own due time." Another two weeks passed. Marilyn could no longer go on living with Carter in her house. Like living with a serial killer, she knew it was only a matter of time before he exploded.

In desperation, Marilyn called a local Columbus attorney and asked if she could meet with him. It took over an hour to explain what her life had been like, particularly for the last five years. A second meeting was scheduled, and a third. Marilyn finally summoned the courage to do what she knew she had to do. She didn't want a divorce, knowing that adultery and death were the only two ways to end a marriage, per Club rules. But she did not want to live with Carter and she did not want him in her house.

When the papers were served and Carter was forced to move out of the house, Marilyn heard from the elders at her Hall immediately. They wanted to meet with her right away. What she had done did not match with the Bible and Club rules. If she expected to stay in good standing with the Club, the elders advised her to take him back. She and Carter should then take this problem to Jehovah and He would help them mend their marriage.

Marilyn again asked, "So what if I take him back and he really does kill me this time, then what?"

Tim responded with, "You will be resurrected in the New World." To him, it was that simple. But Marilyn had the courage to stand up and tell him that option did not sit well with her.

Tim then explained that if she did not take him back, the committee would not be able to disfellowship (DF) her. However, the elders would be obligated to shun her while she attended meetings and in social settings. It would be their way of helping her see God's great wisdom in this matter and their actions would ultimately save her marriage.

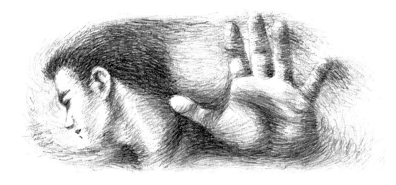

I have never heard of a verdict where shunning was an option without a person being disfellowshipped. I am certain that some-one from Club headquarters advised Tim in this matter. But no one would talk with me about it. So I imagine this decision came from the Club's legal department, concerned about how poorly it would play out in the court of worldly public opinion. Neither Marilyn nor Carter committed adultery. Marilyn did not want to live with Carter, the elders said she couldn't kick him out of the house, and Marilyn did not listen to their advice and used the U.S. court system to remove him.

What happened during the next six months tested Marilyn's faith in the Club as God's agent. When she attended meetings, the elders and their families would not speak to her. They treated her as if she were invisible. Carter also attended all those meetings and was treated as though *he* had been abused. The one exception was my parents. They knew what Carter was like and decided to take a stand. They wouldn't be DF-ed for talking to Marilyn, but their actions were seen as indicating a strong disconnect to having a loving relationship with Jehovah. My father was removed as an elder and told that he could no longer give public talks.

My parents consulted with other respected members in the Club and asked their advice. There was a loophole, if they were willing to use it. By moving to another congregation, one in Central City, forty miles away, the members at the Hall would not shun Marilyn. My father would not be eligible to serve as an elder, but he could worship Jehovah as he saw fit. So plans were made and within three months, Marilyn's house—in spite of Carter's protests—and my parents' house were sold. Marilyn and my parents purchased new homes in Central City and it appeared that the dark side of Carter and the Club were just a bad dream.

These events were shared with me after the fact, and only in dribbles and drabs. Just when I would think, "My God, can this get any worse?" I would learn of new developments. In retrospect, I do not know who I am more appalled with, Carter, the Club or my brother, Tim. Yes, my sister was harmed, but her son and daughter would bear the brunt of the emotional damage.

Mama knows the damage done to Marilyn's children is irreparable but she is able to live with that fact. She believes that in the New World Marilyn's kids will grow back to perfection, their childhood trauma will be forgotten and they will live forever in paradise. They were inconvenienced in this lifetime, but it would be well worth the wait.

Marilyn's Story
Part Two
Chapter 24

When I met Marilyn at her Columbus home in August of 1991, I knew that she and Carter were separated. But I had no idea of the ordeal that she had gone through or would yet encounter.

I called to get directions to Marilyn's house when Helen and I checked into our motel. As we drove to her place, we passed the Kingdom Hall on Highway 81, the same Hall I had attended from 1959 to 1962. Many unpleasant memories flooded my mind and suddenly, I noticed Carter mowing the lawn. He did not see us, but I wondered what he would do if he knew we would soon be meeting and spending time with his children.

Marilyn knew we were coming and stood on her lawn, jumping up and down as we parked the car in front of her house. Tears were streaming down her face. We had been separated for over fourteen years. The joy of that initial hug cannot be put into words, I cry every time I try. Neither of us wanted to let go. Finally, she said, "Please come in. I want you to meet my kids." That, too, was an emotional experience and difficult to write about.

First, I picked up Edith, a plump, smiling little girl, as pleased to see me as I was to see her. Whatever Marilyn had told Edith about me had to be very good. Edith was the spitting image of Marilyn at the same age, just bigger boned. But what concerned me was that she stuttered. No one is born a stutterer. Something had happened, maybe something Carter did.

Marilyn then dragged me into Martin's room. A very handsome boy with curly hair, he looked like I imagined Papa as a child. He knew we were there, but he was more interested in finishing the painting project he was working on. I suspect that we could have walked out of the room and he would not have noticed. But I decided to sit down with him, asking if I could help. He looked up, pleased that I wanted to be his helper. Suddenly, we were friends and he did not want me to leave.

After playing with Martin for ten minutes, I excused myself as I knew Marilyn wanted to show me her house. As she directed the tour, she told me that she had called my parents and Susan. They were on their way, looking forward to seeing me after all these years. They would join us for dinner. I had been excited about connecting with Marilyn, but was still not so sure how I'd feel about meeting with parents who had shunned me for over ten years.

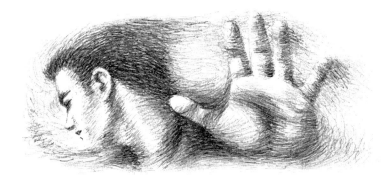

When Mama and Papa walked into the house, they were as excited as I can ever recall. Mama rushed to hug me, saying how happy she was to see me. I looked older, but handsome as ever. Papa seemed just as pleased to see me and kept asking how I was doing. No tears were shed and I had an ambivalent feeling about the whole thing. Mama had told me ten years before that unless I decided to love Jehovah as she did, she would never talk to me again. Now, it was like nothing had ever happened. I did not know why she could greet me or share a meal with me.

I remember eating dinner, a meal Marilyn had worked long and hard to prepare. The over-cooked chicken was hard to chew and tasteless, the vegetables bland, the potato as hard as a rock, and a mediocre salad. It seemed bizarre that Marilyn and my parents still belonged to a cult that advocated not eating a meal with people like Helen and me. At least for one meal, they decided to break the rule, and my God, they could not do better than this?

Our conversation during the meal was nothing more than general chit chat, stuff that works well with strangers, but not with people who were once your immediate family. Marilyn and my parents appeared oblivious to this disconnect. I wanted to have one-on-one conversations with Marilyn and then Mama, and I eventually did, but this kind of talk unnerved me.

When I talked alone with Marilyn, she acknowledged her duplicity in allowing the Club to do her thinking and in shunning me. She didn't say a thing about how poorly she had been treated by Tim and Carter. But I felt her honesty in what we did talk about. We all make mistakes and I had no intention of locking her out of my life because of an error in judgment.

Now, the one-on-one conversation with Mama and my gut check reaction, that's something else altogether. Mama was unable to see the world through any other lens than her own. She had no remorse for anything she had done and gave no explanation of why she decided to share a meal with me or why she could now talk to me. Mama is cold and hard, like talking to a 120-pound block of ice.

The next day while we were at Mama's house talking, Papa picked up the phone in the next room. Carter called to yell at Papa for having the audacity to allow his kids to share a meal with me in the house he owned. He ranted on and on about me, the essence of evil. Papa helped facilitate the crime and he would hear from the elders about this. Marilyn had told me about Carter's obsessive hatred for me, fueled by a cult that had lost its sense of human decency years ago. Carter blamed the failure of their marriage on me. It made no sense, but Carter needed a scapegoat. Papa listened to him talk without responding for nearly fifteen minutes. At the end of his tirade, Papa thanked him for calling and hung up.

Papa interrupted my conversation with Mama to give us a full account of the call. When I interrupted and asked for an explanation, Mama said that Carter could be crazy at times and it was best to let him rant. It was obvious that Mama was getting more upset with each newsy tidbit. Finally, she suggested that I leave. She was tired and they planned to go to the circuit assembly the next day. That's the last time I would talk with Mama before she called me five months later to see how I was doing.

When Helen and I arrived back in Grand Rapids, Marilyn started calling me on the phone two or three times a week. On Saturdays, we talked for as long as two hours. In bits and pieces, I learned about her story. Carter had reported to the elders that his kids shared a meal with me in his home. He wanted some justice and he wanted Marilyn and my parents to be punished. The elders didn't talk to Marilyn about the incident, but they did have words with my parents. What was said, we will never know.

Carter started writing letters to Marilyn, asking for reconciliation, saying she needed help, couldn't she see the damage done to the kids, and more. He cut the power lines to the house once. He disconnected the phone and cable connection several times. Clever enough to make it look like worn wires, he methodically ratcheted his diabolical plan to get her to come back to him.

Marilyn had started to attend a local college in Columbus, a no-no for JWs in good standing with the Club. She planned to get a two-year graduate degree so that she could be a paralegal. She had been reading books about emotional intelligence, psychology, and more. She wanted my opinion on subjects that JWs frowned on. For the first time in her life, she began to think on her own. What a joy for me to be a party to her new world of learning that had for most of her life been taboo. Marilyn started growing as a person and I became her biggest supporter. And the slows, which had so defined Marilyn for so many years, disappeared.

The JW experience for women, especially for girls who grow up in the Club, is nonstop dogma about God using men to lead, teach, decide and govern because they've been gifted with these inalienable rights. A woman's role in the church is subservience to a man's leadership. If she must pray at the Hall or before the door-to-door work, she has to put a covering on her head, be it a hat or a Kleenex tissue, out of respect for the angels watching over her. Little wonder that many JW women have this constant, nagging feeling of inadequacy.

This Ghost of Inadequacy Would No Longer Haunt Marilyn

Marilyn ultimately made a clean break from the Club and Carter. While Carter haunted her by moving across the street when she moved and bought a home in Central City, she persevered. Much can be said about her character and determination during those difficult times. And to give some credit to my parents, they helped Marilyn financially and socially as much as they could, even if it was too little and too late.

But like so many ex-JWs, there were ghosts to pay after breaking free from the Club's clutches. When Marilyn graduated with honors at the community college in Columbus, she rid herself of several ghosts, in particular the ghost of misinformation. But the ghost that would lead to her death, she could not identify or see it coming. Her deadly ghost was the Ghost of Dependency and a fatal attraction to highly controlling men.

This part of her story is very difficult for me to put on paper. So I will try to be short and to the point when I tell you that she married a third time. While the man claimed to be religious, he was not a JW. She attended a local Lutheran church with him and they tried to make a Brady-Bunch family—Marilyn's two kids and his four boys—work. All went well for six months before Marilyn's new husband let his violent nature, his intense need to control, surface.

Marilyn called me a day after it happened. His anger had not been directed at her, but at one of his boys. It scared her and she wanted my advice. Maybe he was having a bad day. He had more temper tantrums but they were always directed at his kids. Then Marilyn became the target for one of his anger attacks. He agreed to go with her to a counselor. But it would be two steps forward, three steps back. Finally, she decided to file for divorce and moved to Grand Island.

While she was alone in her apartment on April 11, 1998, her estranged husband broke into the house. No one knows what was said or how he worked himself in, but before he left, he had knifed my sister to death. The coroner reported ten to fifteen stab wounds to her body.

When my parents didn't hear from Marilyn the next day, they called the police. Three days later, Mama called to tell me the bad news. When I asked about the funeral plans, she said coldly, "Marilyn's been cremated. She's dead and there's nothing we can do about it." Her daughter's brutal murder had little impact on Mama as far as I could see.

Unlike Mama, Marilyn's death strongly affected my life.

For a while, I struggled with unanswerable questions: How do you make sense of a senseless crime? How could anyone hate so much that they are willing to kill, to murder someone? I quickly realized that finding answers would not bring her back. I needed to find a healthy way to bring closure to such a devastating loss.

Soon afterward, I attempted to do something totally out of character, something I had no business doing—I wrote a book, then another. If Marilyn's story could help other people, then I would learn how to write. Perhaps her story, told along with mine and Helen's, would inspire just one person to alter her or his life course, to do something that she or he would not have otherwise done. That is my hope. I could not be happier that I did it. That's what big brothers do.

The End

A Post Script to Marilyn's Story

Marilyn would be alive today if it was up to me and this book would not have been written. But I didn't have a say in the matter. While justice was served when Marilyn's ex pleaded guilty of murder and he was sent to prison, I wanted to do something special to honor Marilyn's life. Writing a book accomplished that and it was good therapy as well. The book also acted as a catalyst for meeting kindred spirits that I now consider members of my extended family. Like Job, I was tested, but I have also been blessed.

One of those blessings is Jennifer Treece. She read my first book, enjoyed it, and wanted to meet me. Jennifer spent eight years at Bethel. While treated better than most women there, she figured out the fatal flaws of the Club. She left Bethel and tried to disappear without any fanfare. When her parents and brother learned that she had stopped going to the meetings, they thought shunning would be the best way to bring her back. They didn't want to see or hear from her until she could love Jehovah, just like them. So Jennifer and I decided to adopt each other as siblings.

In 2009, I participated in the first Tucson Book Festival. I was given a booth to promote *Mama's Club* and paired with Esther Royer Ayers for an hour presentation. She is another one of my adopted sisters. Esther wrote *Rolling Down Black Stockings*, a revealing book about growing up as an Old Order Mennonite. It's amazing how similar Esther's childhood was to me and Marilyn's, all three of us force-fed Kool-Aid, albeit in different flavors.

During our presentation, a very vocal, likeable woman, Melissa Griebel, raised her hand and reported that she had been a JW for thirty years, left the Club five years before. After the meeting, Melissa and I scheduled lunch for the next week. There I learned that Melissa and her JW husband were the parents of two adopted boys, although it wasn't a happy marriage. While she was alone at an insurance convention, she had an epiphany. Her hormones did somersaults and the lights went on: She might be gay! But she thought this overwhelming feeling could be a kidney stone working its way out. So she didn't act on the impulse.

Several weeks later, all the lightbulbs were still on. It wasn't a kidney stone. She also figured out that the Club had been misleading her for years. Melissa broke the news to her husband, gently informed the boys, and was immediately shunned by JW family. Melissa met Sue Dunn eight years ago and it was magic from the start. In fact, it still is.

Helen and I were invited to dinner at Melissa and Sue's place with the boys. Two weeks later, we enjoyed a picnic lunch and walk. Then the four of them came to dinner at our house. Six months later, I can say that Melissa and Sue are two of the most competent parents that I've ever known. So Helen and I unofficially adopted Melissa, Sue and the boys.

Helen and I have developed a close friendship with former next-door neighbors, Charles and Barbara Hedgepeth. They were big supporters of the first book, pushing me to get it into bookstores. Charley would constantly rag on me, "You're taking forever to put *Mama's Club* in print." He worried that he would be dead before the book saw the light of day. My sister Marilyn would have like that.

My step dad died in 2001from prostate cancer. After the funeral, Mama showed Helen and me a pink suit hanging in the closet. She hoped that it would be the first suit Papa wore after being resurrected in the new world.

Mama is 90 years old and in good health. She lives in a government-subsidized-senior-citizens apartment complex. My sister, Susan, is 65 and lives in an assisted living home nearby.

A Post Script to Marilyn's Story

They see each other every day.

Tim and Esther live three miles away and go to the same Kingdom Hall as Mama. The three of them still go in the door-to-door work telling people that Armageddon is imminent, that it will happen in their lifetime.

Our son Keith decided at age eleven that he wanted to be a chemical engineer and today that's what he does for a living in Houston, Texas. Keith is 47, happily married to Amy and they are the proud parents of 16-year-old twins — Hannah and Katrina.

Our daughter Kim is happily married to Jon Waalkes. The two of them designed and built a Rick-Bayless-would-be-envious home in Grand Rapids, Michigan. Along with their daughters, Erika (16) and Annie (13), they are all well-informed, passionate foodies.

Helen and I are happy and doing well. In October 2011, I pulled off a surprise 70th birthday party for her with help from Keith, Kim and Helen's sister, Ellie Kleinheksel. Our friends, Don and Cheryl Brown, hosted the party at their country club.

Three months before, I received a telephone call from Ellie's daughter, Kris Clark. She heard about the party and wanted to know if she and her sister, Kathy Hall, could come. Kris also asked if we could honor her mother as well. Ellie would turn 75 on October 30. And Kris wanted to surprise her mom with a birthday weekend visit. I couldn't let Ellie know they were coming. I'd have to keep two big secrets for several months.

On Friday October 28, the day before Helen's actual birthday, many of our friends and relatives flew in from Michigan, Florida and Texas. In the morning, I told Helen that I had to meet with my publisher. Instead, I met with Kathy and Kris at their hotel. While we were trying to figure out how and when to surprise their mom, Kathy said, "You know, Uncle Dick, I almost didn't get here today."

"What happened?" I asked.

"Well, what happened occurred forty years ago. I use to spend occasional weekends with Grandma Geerling while growing up. She would tell me about Armageddon and a new world. She was so convincing that I started to believe it. That is until my dad learned what Grandma was doing. He went to see her right away.

183

Told her to stop preaching religion to me, or I couldn't spend time with her anymore."

"So, Uncle Dick, if my dad hadn't stepped in, I could have been a JW, and you know they don't believe in birthdays."

We both laughed and decided we'd better get to work on figuring out how we were going to surprise her mom. I would be picking up Ellie and her partner, Herb Olney, at the Tucson airport in less than three hours.

Shortly after lunch, Kathy, Kris and I pulled off the surprise of Ellie's life when Ellie walked into the lounge area at the La Paloma Embassy Suites. But the biggest surprise loomed hours away.

At 5:00 PM, Helen and I picked up Don and Cheryl for what Helen thought would be dinner for four. We small talked driving to the country club. Cheryl kept Helen distracted with more small talk as we slowly worked our way to the third floor ball room. Don opened the door, and there Helen was greeted by her kids, granddaughters, a sister, nieces and many of our friends. This picture, taken by our good friend, Jeff Hershel, tells it all.

My Religious Philosophy

I have received hundreds of letters, emails and comments from readers telling me how much they enjoyed my first book. But what amazes me is how frequently I am asked about my religious beliefs. My publisher says, "Dick, you were so evenhanded in *Growing Up in Mama's Club* that people are naturally curious about your theology."

Their questions vary. Are you a believer? Do you go to church? What church do you go to? Do you believe in God? Are you a Christian? Have you accepted Jesus Christ as your personal savior? These are not difficult questions to answer. But I would like to know what drives people to ask them. Are they looking for me to support their religious convictions?

If someone persists and wants to know my thoughts on religion—God, the Bible and the Hereafter—I quote Joseph Wood Krutch, "The world of poetry, mythology, and religion represent the world as a man would like to have it, while science represents the world as he gradually comes to discover it."

Not that I don't like to talk theology with open-minded people, I thoroughly enjoy talking with people who are searching for the truth. People who say they have found it, well that's another story.

I had an interesting conversation with my friend Merlin Benningfield, who posed the question, "What am I better off believing, that there's a God and a hereafter or atheism?" I'm not certain that's how the question should be asked and I reminded Merlin that good answers can best occur when questions are properly framed. I didn't think his was a good question. But he persevered, reminding me that atheism gets you nothing. When you die, he maintained, you're dead forever. At least a belief in God has more upside to it, cake versus death. But I told him that JWs use a similar type of logic: Would you like to live forever in a new world or die at Armageddon with all the nonbelievers? Is that a good question?

I enjoy talking to people like Merlin because he has an open mind. He and his wife, Sheri, are thinkers, and in our theological journey we will all arrive at different places at different times, many of us looking for the ultimate truth about life, God and the potential for a hereafter.

Deep, theological, *critical* thinkers, like the Episcopalian priest John Shelby Spong, spend the bulk of their time figuring out how to frame questions so they can come up with good answers. This is so unlike Club hierarchy, which asks questions in *The Watchtower* and other literature and then expects people to play back the answers printed conveniently in their magazines and books. Again, is the question a good question? Is it relevant? Who is asking the question and why?

Like my grandfather, I believe that *responsible theology is rooted in what people do and how they live their life*. They can verbally fantasize what they would like to believe. But how does it impact their behavior? And, what are the facts, the data and the science that helped them reach their specific beliefs. This is the kind of stuff that I think about.

For those of you who want to know what I believe, and more to the point, am I a Christian? Yes, I think I am, but probably not like most people define Christianity. Credit it on overexposure from a hardcore cult or maybe I'm on to something.

What happens after we die? I'm not sure. Maybe I will find out some day, or I will fall asleep knowing that my friends and I may have made this planet a better place to live for my grandchildren and great-grandchildren.

My Religious Philosophy

Most readers may want to stop here. You know my life story and my basic beliefs. However, if you need to know more, *at this moment in time*, I believe in God and call myself a Christian, but this needs an explanation.

When I asked a very dear and trusted friend, Bob Rogers, for his advice on *My Religious Philosophy*, here is what he said: "Wow! I really thought you were an atheist. After ripping apart the idea of religion, you then tell us you're a Christian, with caveats? It's a little jarring….the agnostic in me needs to know how you see yourself …."

I mentioned earlier that framing questions is critical if one wants meaningful answers. I also want to add to the mix that *language matters*. Framing one's values and beliefs in the right kind of language is very important to me. [One can't see or hear *frames*, what scientists call the *cognitive unconscious*. Framing is about using language that fits a worldview related to one's beliefs.]

So when people ask if I believe in a God, I confidently use a common frame to tell them *yes*. But my definition of God varies significantly from most Christians. To me, God is a force or energy field, which I cannot fully explain or understand. But He, She or Whatever is responsible for triggering or making life randomly possible. He or this Force also sustains all life. God is bigger and more complex than humans can imagine.

God is not like humans. I believe the God of Moses and Abraham in the Bible is an invention of man. The Bible was written by men who saw God through their lens, with a man's full range of good and bad emotions. God is not a micromanager. He does not need to be worshipped. He doesn't promise life after death. He did not make angels that made themselves into the Devil and his demons. I cannot imagine that God required the death of His son before He would forgive a fallen humanity. That's a portrait of a child abuser. God is not vindictive with judgment, reward, and punishment as His primary modes of behavior.

My ultimate reality is that *I cannot tell anyone who God is or what God is, and neither can anyone else.* The reality of God can never be defined. It can only be experienced, and that experience may be an illusion. When people speak of their experience of

189

God, they can only do it with human analogies, in very human, non-God-like terms.

I also believe that most religions meet a desperate need in the human psyche by defining God in a way that gives the masses a self-created security. But, it isn't real. As religion is often practiced, it doesn't provide genuine security, only its illusion. It is a human-coping device designed to create security in a radically insecure world.

Analyze most religious systems and you will discover that they contain two specific divisions. First: What is the proper way to worship to gain God's favor? Second: What's the proper way to behave or live to gain God's approval? From this, I deduce that most human religious systems have never been primarily a search for truth; they are a search for security.

In spite of that, I see myself as a Christian, a John-Spong Christian. About himself he said, "Being a Christian is not to be a religious being; it is to be a whole human being. Jesus is a portrait of that wholeness and why he is for me, in his complete humanity, the ultimate expression of God."

As a child, one of my heroes was Jesus Christ. I didn't see Jesus the way Mama and fundamentalist Christians see him. To me Jesus personified love, not judgment. He was the kind of person I wanted to emulate. He called people to step beyond rules, defenses, tribal boundaries, prejudices and even religion to embrace a full, happy life.

Jesus' attitude toward religion resonated with me. He broke religious boundaries again and again. Any program or doctrine that puts limits on humanity, anything that teaches one to hate, exclude, reject or violate another, cannot be from a humane God. That is what Jesus said in a thousand ways, that religious rules are immoral unless they enhance human life.

Dietrich Bonhoeffer said that humanity would *come of age* when it parted ways with the external, supernatural, parental God of theistic religion. It would mark the dawning of a new day in human consciousness and for it he coined the phrase, "religionless Christianity."

John Shelby Spong sums it up well for me in his book, *Jesus for the Non-Religious*: "The call of Jesus is not a call to be religious. It is not a call to escape life's traumas, to find security, to possess peace of mind. The call of God through Jesus is a call to be fully human, to embrace insecurity without building protective fences, to accept the absence of peace of mind as a requirement of humanity. It is to see that God is the experience of life, love and being who is met at the edges of expanded humanity."

That makes sense to me. Ridding myself of the ghosts from Mama's Club was my starting point. Now, I wish my reader well in his or her journey to make life meaningful and happy.

Having shared my personal beliefs about religion, I want the reader to know that I do not want to proselytize my beliefs. I have many friends and extended family that profess a deep faith in God and it works for them. They live in personal and social integrity and are not haunted by the ghosts that authoritarian and mind-control groups are typically beset with. They read the Bible and they love life, learning, science and people. In other words, their beliefs positively impact their behavior

There are in fact faith traditions, yes religions, which at their best, are commitments to live with integrity in this world, and with a responsibility to society to build its structures and individuals into units of peace and justice. To the few streams of Christian faith that have successfully done this, I openly acknowledge that Jehovah's Witnesses are an aberration.

Questions & Observations from Readers

What happened to Marilyn's two children after she was murdered?

The court awarded Carter, the biological father custody of Marilyn's two children. He continued to raise them as JWs and forbid them from having any relationship with me or Helen. While they are now adults, they would have hell to pay for from the Club and Carter if they were to make contact with me today.

For what it's worth, I think reading "Growing Up in Mama's Club" first makes "The Ghosts from Mama's Club" a smoother, more satisfying read.

Did your father-in-law feel excluded from a social scene that he might have enjoyed had he been allowed to join in?

No, he was happy within himself. Unlike Helen, he was not a social person by nature.

I am curious to know how Club members dealt on a day-to-day basis with non-member spouses and children of members.

If a person is married to a disfellowshipped person, they are able to eat and talk with the spouse. But they are not allowed to discuss religion. If parents have an under-age child who is disfellowshipped, they are not allowed to eat with them. If the child is an adult, he or she must be shunned.

I would like to know about how your brother thinks. He is obviously an intelligent person. I find it amazing that he can't see through the fog.

Even as child Tim wasn't curious about the world he lived in. He had polio at age five and did not live at home for six months and that may have impacted his thinking as an adult. Tim also had high compliance needs and was uncomfortable questioning Club beliefs. He had his doubts, but he suppressed them. In the end, he made a choice (whether he will admit that or not) to allow someone else to do his thinking. In his case, the cult defined who he is.

I would like to know what changed your wife's mind to get you back together since she was so religious. Why would a person continue to go to a church that shunned and banned her husband? Surely there is some kind o lesson to be learned from it. And what was your wife's reasoning which enabled you to both bond together again?

My wife Helen's response is: "I had hoped this book would explain my state of mind as a JW. But if you insist, I love the guy. I never wanted our marriage to break up. And the truth is: I have never been religious. I wanted to please my mother all those years. Okay, I honestly thought it was the truth, to have my cake and eat it too.

"When Dick told me he wanted out of our marriage, I was shocked into reality. I had to give a little if I was going to save it. When I first met the guy, I knew he had potential. I believed he could do anything he made his mind up to do. He was a leader, a good dad, a strong, caring person, the kind of person I wanted in my life.

"I know now that I was slowly and thoroughly brainwashed during my JW years. When the Club announced that my husband must be shunned, I can offer no explanation as to why I didn't react quicker and more aggressively. I still thought it was the truth, but those thoughts were gradually chiseled away with the reality that the Club is not about love and preserving family.

"The lesson to be learned from my story is that every person needs to be able to think on their own and to be very cautious about getting involved with organized religion, particularly the fundamentalist variety. If a person insists on joining a church, she must never sacrifice her thinking skills and needs to question everything without being made to feel guilty."

What line of thinking enabled you to bond with your wife again?

For me, I saw a change in Helen's attitude after we separated. I knew that I wanted to give it a second chance if she was willing to take me back. I also focused more on what made our relationship work and less time on what didn't work.

I strongly believe that change does not occur without some level of conflict. Our separation was the crisis that both Helen and I needed to reevaluate our marriage.

There was a lot heartbreak and sadness in your life, and still you found a way to overcome. I would like to know how you were able to get through your sister's death, the hurt caused by your parents, your JW friends and other relatives who shunned you. What brought you through this?

I could have moaned and groaned and said, "Woe is me." But that would not have changed a thing. The only thing I can control is my beliefs about events over which I have no control. I found comfort in V. Frankl's *Man's Search for Meaning* and Dale Carnegie's work on positive thinking. I also busied myself by helping other people, making new friends and continually learning new things about the world I live in.

I liked the summary of your ghosts, although I wonder if there's a subset of the Ghost of Indignation, which I call intellectual irresponsibility or willful stupidity. This affects the person who is intelligent, curious and skeptical about the underlying logic of the Cult. Once his questioning spirit is unleashed and he lashes out at the Club, he may be haunted as well by the question of why it took so long and a nagging doubt about whether he has the intellectual underpinning to dispassionately search for the truth. The phenomenon is not unique to the disillusioned JW. The Jesuits believe that if you give them a child until he is seven, they will give you the man. During my college years, I worked one summer with a young forester who had had just that growing-up experience in a Jesuit school. Doubts developed, but he repeatedly suppressed them. It wasn't until he had a near-death experience in which the hospital's Protestant doctor kicked out the priest giving him his last rites so that the doctor could get on with saving his life, that the doubts were erased and he left the Church. In our chats, he was not vindictive, but was more frustrated at the time that he had wasted by not more quickly following his intellectual curiosity to its inevitable outcome.

I'm curious to know if the leaders at Bethel had any academic qualifications other than total immersion in the Cult dogma.

The leaders are uneducated with zero academic credentials, believing that God prefers to share His most innermost thoughts with unlettered men. They also embrace **Scientific Ignorance Makes Perfect Sense**, meaning Bethel leaders are proud to have never studied the scientific history of the Bible, astronomy, cosmology, physics, chemistry, biology, or geology. They also have never read any of the tens of thousands of peer-reviewed scientific papers describing the evidence for (1) Big Bang Theory, (2) Abiogenesis, and (3) The Theory of Evolution. While they don't know that these three entirely separate theories have nothing to do with atheism, it still qualifies them to describe these three fields of science as Devil-based knowledge."

I would like to know how Marilyn could be married three times when Club policy stated that only adultery and death dissolved a marriage.

Marilyn's first husband remarried after the annulment, freeing her to marry Carter. Marilyn was celibate for many years after she divorced Carter. She dissociated herself from the Club in 1993 and dated several men before she married her third husband.

Are there other books that people, more comfortable learning new things within a biblical framework, can read after leaving a cult?

Yes. I asked my cousin, Ron Stansell, who has devoted his

entire life to the Christian ministry and practices what he preaches, to suggest books that he would recommend. As an alternative to my list in chapter 14, Ron believes that reading the following books could help readers grasp new information to help them dispel the misinformation experienced in a cult.

1. *Embraced. Prodigals at the Cross* by Steve Sherwood (Eugene, Oregon: Wipf & Stock, 2010). A focus on the ultimate meaning of life, and issues of concern like purpose in life, how life goes wrong, and the hope found in God. Sherwood urges the reader to consider more than one perspective on scripture, the atonement and the nature of the human predicament.

2. *Mere Christianity: Shepherd Notes* by C.S. Lewis (Nashville: Broadman & Holman, 1999). Lewis presents a classical argument for Christian faith as something reasonable and practical, without prescribing answers to every possible kind of theological or biblical questions. He asks the skeptic to reconsider what Jesus claimed to be and how reasonable those claims might be.

3. N. T. Wright, *Simply Jesus* (New York: HarperCollins, 2011). Wright is a scholar and academic but invites believers to discover a new and understandable vision of who Jesus was, what he did and why he matters.

4. Scot McKnight, *The Blue Parakeet: Rethinking How You Read the Bible* (Grand Rapids: Zondervan, 2008). McKnight wants the devout reader of the Bible to go beyond a simplistic reading. One primary emphasis is how we come to answers, rather than the Bible answers themselves. He writes to open minds to new possibilities, not the way many Americans have always heard the Bible described.

5. Alister and Joanna McGrath, *The Dawkins Delusion* (Downers Grove: InterVarsity Press, 2007). The McGraths argue for a serious intellectual engagement with those who oppose them rather than a brusque and thoughtless dismissal of a writer like Dawkins. Alister McGrath holds an Oxford degree in molecular biophysics. Alister and Joanna McGrath are not "easy" reading, but they try to take the physical sciences seriously in their quest for meaning in life.

Is there a good book about the Club's leaders and how they make decisions?

Yes. I would recommend reading *The Four Presidents of the Watchtower Society* by Ed Gruss, in particular chapter 7.

Meeting the Ghosts from Mama's Club

I would like to formally introduce you to the *six ghosts* identified in this book.

To depict *The Ghost of Misinformation*, four manifestations of this ghost are illustrated spewing out toxic, bad information: "God doesn't want you to celebrate your birthday because it takes glory away from Him; God is going to destroy you at Armageddon if you pledge allegiance to the flag or take a blood transfusion; God works only with JWs, the Devil controls all other religions; Christmas is bad and an invention of the devil."

The Ghost of Separation is the second ghost. The main manifestation is *shunning*. The first picture is of the act of shunning and the second is the negative impact on the person shunned. This ghost can be deadly at times. Many ex-JWs commit suicide after being shunned by family and friends.

The third illustration demonstrates the impact of separation anxiety on someone trying to leave the Club.

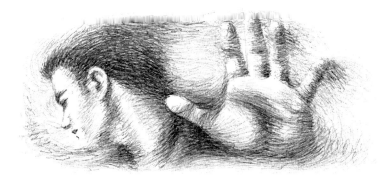

Shunning is Considered Good-Christian Behavior by JWs

Being Shunned is the Reason why many Ex-JWs Commit Suicide

Unable to Bring Closure to One's JW Experience

The Ghost of Inadequacy is the third ghost with six illustrations. This ghost manifests itself when ex-JWs find they are unable to think for themselves and unable to articulate well-thought-out beliefs about God, the Bible and life after death. This ghost also traps its victims with a nagging feeling of inadequacy, particularly women who are treated as second-class citizens by the Club.

Unable to Think for Oneself

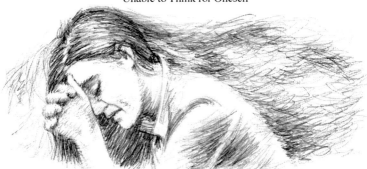

Unable to Think for Oneself

Unable to Articulate Well-Thought-Out Beliefs

A Nagging Feeling of Inadequacy, Especially by Women

The Ghost of Dependency is the fourth ghost with six illustrations. This ghost manifests itself in many shapes and forms, but its goal is to keep the victim in a child-like state of dependence. The Club is Daddy, the Club knows all and members and ex-JWs must never forget that. This ghost's job is to make sure that ex-JWs cannot grow and blossom as productive human beings.

Unable to Assimilate into Mainstream Society

Unable to Assimilate into Mainstream Society

A Need to Control & Put Down Other People as Club Leaders Do

A Lack of Self-Control Because the Person Left the Club's Protection

A Lack of Self-Control because this Person never Learned to be Self-Sufficient

An Attraction to High-Control Religious Groups after Leaving the Club

The Ghost of Indignation is the fifth ghost. Club members are taught that righteous indignation is getting upset with the false teachings of the Catholic Church, man-made governments that reject Jehovah God, etc. So when people leave the Club, they often go on crusades, blaming the Club needlessly for their own complicity—unable to take any responsibility for once going along with the Club's rules and constraints. These crusades result in a lot of wasted energy, as the Club exists because there will always be groups of people who are attracted to high-control religion.

Blaming the Club for One's Complicity

Obsessive Time Spent Trying to Topple the Club

Trying to Bring Down the Club

The Ghost of Guilt is the sixth ghost. Many people have been so well programmed that when they try to leave the Club, they are plagued with a constant feeling of guilt.

The next ghost is a spoof—Casper the friendly ghost if you will. It is *Underlining Key Points in Books and Magazines*. It's learned behavior from underlining answers to the questions in *The Watchtower*. Well, it's harmless learned behavior unless the books and magazines come from the library or friends.

So there you have it, the six ghosts of Mama's Club and twenty-three manifestations— illustrations—thanks to the creative genius of Dan Sharp.

CPSIA information can be obtained at www.ICGtesting.com
Printed in the USA
LVOW081557240812

295831LV00012B/9/P